GIRT

THE UNAUTHORISED HISTORY OF AUSTRALIA

Volume I: From Megafauna to Macquarie

DAVID HUNT

ILLUSTRATIONS BY AD LONG

Published by Black Inc.,
an imprint of Schwartz Media Pty Ltd
37–39 Langridge Street
Collingwood VIC 3066 Australia
email: enquiries@blackincbooks.com
http://www.blackincbooks.com

National Library of Australia Cataloguing-in-Publication entry
Hunt, David, 1971-
Girt : the unauthorised history of Australia / David Hunt.
9781863956116 (paperback)
Includes index.
Australia--History. Australian wit.
Australia--Anecdotes.
994

Book design by Peter Long
Typeset by Duncan Blachford

Contents

For those who've come across the seas

Australian history is almost always picturesque;
indeed, it is so curious and strange, that it is itself the
chiefest novelty the country has to offer and so
pushes the other novelties into second and third place.
It does not read like history, but like the most
beautiful lies; and all of a fresh new sort, no mouldy old
stale ones. It is full of surprises and adventures, and
incongruities, and contradictions, and incredibilities;
but they are all true, they all happened.

MARK TWAIN, *FOLLOWING THE EQUATOR*, 1897.

If an historian were to relate truthfully all the crimes,
weaknesses and disorders of mankind, his readers
would take his work for satire rather than for history.

PIERRE BAYLE, *HISTORICAL AND CRITICAL DICTIONARY*, 1697.

It's funny because it's true.

HOMER SIMPSON, 1991.

Introduction

Our home is girt by sea.

Advance Australia Fair,
Peter Dodds McCormick, 1878

G IRT. NO WORD COULD BETTER CAPTURE THE essence of Australia. Switzerland, Paraguay and Burkina Faso are merely girt by other countries, but Australia is entirely and defiantly girt by sea.

No other nation can rival Australia for sheer maritime girtitude. Australia dwarfs its nearest rival, Greenland, by a girt factor of 3.52 (7,617,930 square kilometres to Greenland's puny 2,166,086). And Greenland isn't even a proper country, just a forlorn Danish outpost that reeks of pickled herring.

Australia justifiably celebrates its girtuosity in its national anthem, for the history of this wide brown land has been shaped by the even wider blue seas in which it rests. It was the warm currents of the Timor Sea that carried the First Australians to these shores, and it was Australia's phenomenal girtage that kept these hardy pioneers blissfully unaware of trousers, smallpox, large mining companies, Shane Warne and the other trappings of Western civilisation for tens of millennia.

It was the vast reaches of the Pacific and Indian Oceans that led Europe's greatest minds to conclude that so much water must be girting something – for surely the world would tip from its axis in the absence of a Great Southern Land to balance the sprawling continents of the northern hemisphere. It was those same dark, churning waters that led the captains of Europe's finest fleets, searching in vain for the elusive southern continent, to ask, "So where the bloody hell are you?"

But *Terra Australis* could not remain *Incognita* forever. The veil of waters parted for Willem Janszoon, Abel Tasman, William Dampier, James Cook, Matthew Flinders and Jessica Watson, revealing a land of golden beaches, storm-kissed bays and jewelled harbours.

And while the world's other great powers saw Australia's unparalleled girtedness as an excellent reason to steer clear of the joint, Britain saw it as a virtue, for it needed a place to stash all its pickpockets, sheep thieves and Irishmen. Britain fervently hoped that the tyranny of distance and the despotism of lots of water would prevent its undesirables from walking back to London.

Australia's isolation made it a giant Petri dish, able to grow a unique culture. It attracted no-hopers, ne'er-do-wells, political prisoners, religious refugees, free thinkers and eccentrics. It drew adventurers and risk-takers and called to the poor, the disadvantaged and the merely socially embarrassing. It served as a bright beacon to a tsunami of opportunists, gamblers, entrepreneurs and gladhanders. Australian ports provided a gateway for sailors and fortune-seekers from all corners of the globe, and the lure of riches or men with big sticks carried the Chinese and Kanaks to our shores.

Australia was the place to be. Unless you were black. Or a woman. Or gay. Or suspected of being Irish. Or even worse, all of the above.

Yet geography, economy and necessity forced Australia's disparate peoples into contact with each other, elevating men of low birth to greatness and lowering a fair share of the mighty. Rich and poor, black and white, gay and straight, Catholic and Protestant and Jew were left to simmer in the cultural melting pot.

In time, a new and distinct people emerged from Britain's colonial kitchen. A people who bathed regularly. A people who liked a bet, a drink and a smoke. A people who were good at ball games. A people who fought and died for whatever Britain or America wanted them to fight and die for and who laughed in the face of Johnny Turk, Uncle Tojo and anyone else who looked or spoke funny. A people who would push technology to its very limits, gifting humanity with the finest lawnmowers and clotheslines the world had ever seen and a strange brown paste that could transform a simple piece of toast into a simple piece of toast covered in a strange brown paste. A people who called themselves Australians.

While our identity evolved, the sea remained a constant. The first three governors of New South Wales were all naval men, which explains why rum, sodomy and the lash have played such an important role in Australian life. Sir Henry Parkes, the man who led the fight for an independent Australia and a poet of outstanding mediocrity, wrote in 1889:

God girdled[1] our majestic isle
With seas far-reaching east and west,
That man might live beneath this smile
In peace and freedom ever blest.

Alfred Deakin, Australia's second prime minister, finished his great 1898 speech in support of Australian federation with the words:

For God has made her one: complete she lies
Within the unbroken circle of the skies,
And round her indivisible the sea
Breaks on her single shore.[2]

Robert Menzies yearned for the love of a blue-hatted woman who lived far over the sea. Malcolm Fraser lost his trousers on the other side of the sea. John Howard and Julia Gillard told people to go back across the sea. And Harold Holt, our greatest submaritime politician, has been girt by sea since 1967.

This is the story of a land and a people who always have been, and always will be, girt. This is the story of us.

---

1   The poem would have been better if Parkes had gone with "girtled".

2   Deakin wasn't going to let Tasmania get in the way of a good speech.

I

For those who've come across the seas

We've boundless plains to share

**Advance Australia Fair,
Peter Dodds McCormick, 1878**

THE VERY LATE CAPTAIN COOK

I T IS THE 29TH OF APRIL 1770 AND CAPTAIN James Cook, the greatest explorer of his age,[1] strides across the deck of the HMS *Endeavour* while his pet botanist, Joseph Banks, scurries in his wake wittering on about seedpods. But Cook only has ears for the siren song of the land that lies spread before him like a welcoming lover. He has discovered her and all her secrets – and this day, at Botany Bay, he will name her and claim her for God, King and Great Britain.

This is, of course, complete nonsense.

---

1   He was forty-two.

Captain Cook wasn't even Captain Cook in 1770, but Lieutenant Cook, a junior officer of no particular note. He arrived between 60,000 and 164 years too late to discover Australia (depending on whom you listen to) and claimed the continent's entire east coast, which he didn't like much, on Possession Island in the Torres Strait, naming it New Wales[2] because it reminded him very much of sunny tropical Wales.

By the time Cook got around to not discovering Australia, Spanish eyes had gazed upon her emerald rainforests, a Dutch psychopath had bathed her beaches in the blood of his countrymen, and her northern shores had serviced China's sexually adventurous and erectilely challenged for at least half a century.

So what of those who came across the sea before Cook? They certainly didn't tell of boundless plains to share. The general consensus was that Australia was sandy, boring and full of hostile savages who weren't interested in buying tea.

THE FIRST ENGLISHMAN
NOT TO DISCOVER AUSTRALIA

Cook wasn't even the first Englishman not to discover Australia. That honour fell to the murderously incompetent Captain John Brookes in 1622.

Brookes was one of the first children of a new golden age in which the English dreamt of empire. King James VI of Scotland had ascended the English throne in 1603, joining

---

2   Cook added the "South" bit later. New South Wales just had a better ring to it.

the two previously hostile countries together under a common monarch and changing his name to King James I. The Irish were crushed in the same year, after sixty years of war and an even longer period of jokes at their expense. The English jackboot had already trampled the Welsh daffodil and the much hardier leek and, with Scotland and Ireland now subdued, a truly great Britain was looking to make her mark on the wider world. Britain's first permanent colony was established in 1607 and, when the *Mayflower* pilgrims went to starve and freeze in America in 1620, Britain was well on her way to becoming a great colonial power. [3]

But in 1622 Britannia did not yet rule the waves, with the Spanish, Dutch and French fleets challenging her naval supremacy. And while Great Britain is now a nation of shopkeepers, back then if Brookes wanted to buy a really good cheese, tulip, painting of a chubby nude chick with red hair or, most importantly, the latest must-have condiment, he would have had to ask the Dutch.

Europe had discovered that its traditional cuisine of turnip and lard was actually edible when heavily disguised with spices. Pepper was all the rage, the landed gentry held nutmeg parties, and gold was worth its weight in cloves. Most of these exotic treats could only be found in the East Indies (now Indonesia) and the Dutch East India Company held the keys to the spice rack.

And so it is we find Captain Brookes of the *Tryall* skulking off the North West Cape of Western Australia, en route

---

3   The British were delightfully impractical colonists. The *Mayflower* didn't carry fripperies like seeds or livestock, but one of its passengers, William Mullins, thoughtfully packed 139 pairs of shoes to starve in.

to the East Indies, his hold full of silver to buy pepper from under the noses of the Dutch.

In fairness to Captain Cook, he knew he had run into Australia (or New Holland, as it was then known). Brookes had no idea. When Brookes sighted the Australian coast, he thought it a small island in the Indian Ocean. This was his first navigational mistake. His second was to run his ship into a small island in the Indian Ocean, which he thought to be open sea. The low-lying island, now known as Tryal Rocks, lies about 100 kilometres off the West Australian coast and is the site of the first proven European shipwreck in Australian waters.

Historians spend a lot of time doing useful things like debating the meaning of the word "discovery". The consensus is that running into something without realising where it is does not constitute discovery, although this rule is not applied to Christopher Columbus, who maintained until his dying day that he had crashed into Asia and that America did not exist. [4] Another rule of discovery is that you must leave X, find Y, and then return to X and announce, "I have just found Y." You can't stay in Y being hand-fed papaya by the sixty Polynesian virgins who have declared you to be a living god.

So Brookes saw Australia, Brookes crashed into Australia, but Brookes did not "discover" Australia. [5]

---

4   Columbus was also one of history's most inept spice traders. The overrated mariner, incorrectly believing himself to be in Asia, painstakingly scraped away at some West Indian trees that he incorrectly believed to be cinnamon. When he arrived back in Spain, he proudly showed off his cargo of useless bark.

5   Brookes also did not discover Australia because the Dutch and a whole lot of other people got there before him.

Brookes was not the sort of captain to go down with his ship. He was, however, the sort of captain to make off with its silver while his men drowned around him. Brookes and forty-five of his crew escaped in the ship's longboat and skiff, which had room for many more men, leaving ninety-three of their fellows to succumb to hunger, thirst and high tide. He made it to Batavia (modern-day Jakarta) and told his employer, the British East India Company, that all its silver was lying at the bottom of the Indian Ocean. He promised that he had stuck to his allocated course and had been nowhere near New Holland. For centuries, sea-men searched the wrong seas for the *Tryall*'s treasure. Only in 1969 was the wreck discovered and the first sighting of Australia by an Englishman confirmed.

THE FIRST ENGLISH BACKPACKER

The next Englishman not to discover Australia was William Dampier. Dampier was England's first professional tourist and clocked up a phenomenal quantity of frequent-sailor points, being the first man to circumnavigate the globe three times.

Dampier was also a pirate, but he was a sensitive pirate with soulful eyes and long girly hair who kept a diary in which he recorded his feelings about the many lands, people, plants and animals he encountered. Dampier's pirating gave him an opportunity to see the world and kill all sorts of new and interesting people, although, in his defence, he felt bad about it afterwards (unless his victims were Spanish).

The pirates of the Caribbean, of which Dampier was one, had many endearing qualities. They revived the democracy of the ancient Greeks, with crew members electing their captain and voting on where to travel and whom to kill. After an honest day's raping and pillaging, they would divide the day's spoils equally. They introduced the world's first workers' compensation scheme, with payouts determined by battle-wound severity.[6] On the island of Tortuga, buccaneers lived in lifelong male pairs; partners were known as *matelots* and they did, sharing property, food, a bed and, in every sense of the word, each other's booty. The English turned a blind eye to this bohemian lifestyle because the pirates were awfully good at burning Spanish towns, sinking Spanish ships and hanging Spanish sailors from the yardarm by their entrails, all of which the English regarded as jolly good sport.

So in 1688 we find William Dampier pirating off the Mexican coast aboard Captain Swan's *Cygnet*.[7] Swan was tired of killing Spaniards in the Americas and suggested to his crew that they might like to kill some different Spaniards in the Philippines. Dampier wrote that the crew of the *Cygnet* only had three days' worth of rations by the time they reached Guam and "had contrived to kill Captain Swan and eat him when the victuals were gone". Although Swan escaped undevoured, the *Cygnet*'s Asian booty was restricted to rice and cotton, a far cry from the gold and silver of the Americas.

---

6   The generous compensation scheme enabled maimed pirates to buy wooden legs, fitted hooks, eye patches, etc. There is no historical evidence of a parrot allowance.

7   "The little swan" – this is an example of pirate humour.

The *Cygnet* was now being hunted by the Spanish and the crew voted to lie low in New Holland for a while on the grounds that everyone said the place was a dump; no one in their right mind could think the English would ever go there. And so, on 4 January 1688,[8] Dampier landed on the coast of Western Australia. His diary from his short stay shows that, like many Englishmen abroad, he didn't like the climate, the people or the food. He wrote:

> The inhabitants of this country are the miserablest people in the world. The Hodmadods of Monomatapa, though a nasty people, yet for wealth are gentlemen to these; who have no houses, and skin garments, sheep, poultry, and fruits of the earth, ostrich eggs, etc., as the Hodmadods have: and, setting aside their human shape, they differ but little from brutes ... They are long-visaged, and of a very unpleasing aspect, having not one graceful feature in their faces.

After getting Anglo–Aboriginal relations off to such a promising start, Dampier left our shores, bought a tattooed East-Indian slave named Jeoly, returned to England, sold Jeoly to a travelling freak show, and published the diary of his travels. *A New Voyage Round the World* was, with the exception of the Bible, the most popular book of its era – part seventeenth-century Lonely Planet guide, part

---

8   This is 4 January 1689 under the modern calendar. Until 1752 the English celebrated New Year's Day on 25 March, the day Mary conceived Jesus (Lady's Day). When the English adopted the Gregorian calendar they celebrated New Year's Day on 1 January, the day Jesus was circumcised (Small Screaming Boy's Day).

swashbuckling potboiler. Dampier could move seamlessly from a botanical description of the banana[9] to a dissertation on the sexual mores of Filipino women, before launching into tales of rapine upon the high seas and enumerating the many failings of the various foreigners he had met and killed.

Dampier traded off his literary success and came up with a daring new plan. He would join the Royal Navy and go not discover Australia again!

The voyage was a disaster. His ship, the *Roebuck*, leaked and, to the horror of its sodden sailors, ran out of beer. By the time the *Roebuck* arrived in Western Australia, her crew were losing their teeth to scurvy[10] and had nominated Dampier "Mr World's Worst Captain 1699".

Dampier again damned Australia with faint praise:

> If it were not for that sort of pleasure which results from the discovery of even the barrenest spot upon the globe, the coast of New Holland would not have charmed me much.

Dampier averted mutiny by agreeing to take his disgruntled crew home, abandoning his mission just 100 miles from Australia's east coast.

Dampier's *A Voyage to New Holland* was another literary success and ensured continued English interest in the

---

9   Dampier believed the banana to be "the king of all fruit", rating the plantain slightly above the dessert banana.

10 Scurvy is a vitamin-C deficiency, with symptoms including blackened skin, swollen and bleeding gums, tooth loss, extremely bad breath, uncontrollable crying and dropping dead in agony. It commonly affected sailors who were deprived of fresh food on long sea voyages, with as many as two million seamen dying from the disease between 1500 and 1850 A.D.

continent. His descriptions of Australia's unpleasant wildlife – he disliked all the sharks and snakes and declared the shingleback lizard the ugliest creature he had ever seen – would inspire future generations of naturalists, including Sir Joseph Banks and Charles Darwin. Yet Dampier's most lasting contribution has been to literature and the English language. His voyages inspired Jonathan Swift's *Gulliver's Travels*, [11] and the desert island abandonment of Alexander Selkirk, one of his sailing companions, was the inspiration for Daniel Defoe's *Robinson Crusoe*. Dampier's writings introduced albatross, avocado, breadfruit, cashew, chopsticks, dildo-bush, [12] posse, subspecies and tortilla into the English vocabulary.

William Dampier is undoubtedly one of the greatest Englishmen never to have discovered Australia.

MAKE LOVE, NOT LANDFALL

While English exploration was motivated by dreams of empire, the French came to the southern seas as an intellectual exercise. The mathematician and philosopher Pierre-Louis Moreau du Maupertuis suggested twelve projects for the French advancement of human knowledge, one of which was the exploration of the southern hemisphere.

---

11   Swift wrote that the country of Lilliput was "to the north-west of Van Diemen's Land" (Tasmania), which explains why South Australians are shorter than other Australians.

12   Strangely, this name for a suggestively shaped Caribbean cactus has never really taken off. Dampier did not introduce the word "dildo" into the English lexicon, this honour being claimed by Shakespeare in *A Winter's Tale*.

The French believed they had been chosen by Destiny to reveal great new southern lands to an awestruck world, fire the spark of civilisation in the noble savage's breast, and make wild passionate love to women who had never before experienced the intoxicating scent of garlic laced with stale *Gitanes*.

Louis-Antoine de Bougainville, inspired by du Maupertuis, explored the South Pacific in 1766, during his effort to become the first Frenchman to circumnavigate the globe. It was hoped that the voyage would restore the honour of glorious France, which had ended the Seven Years' War with yet another demonstration of its unrivalled expertise in surrendering. This was also the first voyage of discovery to carry a cargo of *les geeks* to methodically probe small furry animals and collect interesting rocks. Among these men of learning were the botanist Philibert Commerçon (who sucked up to his boss by naming the bougainvillea) and Jean Baré, his boyish assistant and frequent below decks companion.

In 1767, de Bougainville named Tahiti *Nouvelle Cythera* after the island of Aphrodite, the Greek Goddess of Love. Describing Tahiti in his steamy *Voyage autour du monde*, Bougainville offered a vision of an earthly paradise where men were men and women were easy, inspiring generations of French intellectuals, artists and perverts to pack their bags for Polynesia.

While the French thought they knew about women, the Tahitians got one up on them. As soon as they met Jean Baré, they burst out laughing and identified "him" as Jeanne Baré. Commerçon had packed his mistress and this arrangement had gone unnoticed for over four months.

Jeanne became the first woman to circumnavigate the globe, although those who like to belittle female achievement point out that she did half of it as a man. [13]

After leaving Tahiti, Bougainville discovered Samoa (which had earlier been discovered by the Dutch) and Vanuatu (which had earlier been discovered by the Spanish). While searching for the mythical *Terre Australie*, [14] Bougainville came within sight of the Great Barrier Reef, leading some diehard French nationalists to claim that the French discovered the east coast of Australia. However, the truth is that Bougainville, when confronted by the reef, responded in typical French fashion. He ran away.

IS THAT A SLUG IN YOUR POCKET?

For centuries, Makassan traders from the Indonesian island of Sulawesi had been harvesting sea cucumbers (trepang) on the north Australian coast. The sea cucumber's value lay in it being prized by the Chinese as an aphrodisiac.

The sea cucumber appears an odd choice of marital aid as it is not remotely sexy, except perhaps to another sea cucumber. It is a large, black, slug-like creature that spends its entire life sitting in shallow water, aspiring to nothing more than avoiding ending up in a Beijing sex shop.

---

13   Other French explorers adopted Commerçon's tactics. For example, Louis de Freycinet dressed his wife as a man and smuggled her aboard his voyage to Australia in 1817. He then needed seventeen men (real ones) to guard her virtue from the crew, who had not so thoughtfully packed for three years at sea. Rose de Freycinet, like Jeanne Baré, went on to circumnavigate the globe.

14   Everyone else called it *Terra Australis*, but the French refused to speak anything other than French.

The Makassans were the first non-Aboriginal people to settle in Australia for any length of time, with up to forty ships and over 1,000 men coming to northern Australia each trepang season. Makassan divers would collect tonnes of the Viagra slugs and deliver them to demountable factories on shore, where they would be boiled, dried, buried in sand for weeks, dug up, boiled again and then smoked. [15]

The Makassans had a profound impact on the culture, language [16] and economies of the Yolngu of Arnhem Land and other Aboriginal peoples they encountered. They exchanged cloth, tobacco, knives, rice and alcohol for the right to harvest trepang and hire local labour – the earliest record of trade between Aborigines and the outside world.

Indonesian fishermen have been coming to Australia in search of trepang and other less sexy sea-life for centuries. Now we burn their boats. This is called progress.

THE LAND THAT GOD PASSED BY

The Spanish would certainly have colonised Australia, had they bothered to land there. As it was, they were too busy avoiding the cannibals to the north, who showed no interest in being redeemed for Christ and altogether too much interest in using Spanish skulls as novelty table ornaments.

On 3 October 1606, Luís Vaz de Torres was sailing

---

15   Readers who think this sounds erotic are encouraged to take a cold shower and seek professional help.

16   For example, the Yolngu called the white people they had never seen *balanda*, a corruption of Hollander.

through the strait that now bears his name. If Torres had taken the time to check out the land visible a few miles to the south, his countryman, Juan Antonio Samaranch, would never have had cause to mispronounce, "And the winner is Syd-er-ney". Sydney would have instead been named Santa Kylie or San Wazza and its residents would now be taking regular afternoon naps.

The Spanish, the world's pre-eminent imperialists, had three interests in exploring the South Seas: discovering *Terra Australis Incognita*, discovering gold and silver, and discovering new Catholics. [17]

Terra Australis Incognita, the "Unknown South Land", was invented by the Greek philosopher Aristotle. Pythagoras, who is still hated by schoolkids for making triangles more complex than they need to be, had earlier determined that the earth was spherical. Aristotle took Pythagoras's idea and ran with it. He knew there was a lot of land in the northern hemisphere and reasoned that there must be a similar amount in the undiscovered south to prevent the globe from tipping over. Aristotle had just brilliantly demonstrated that logic is a very dangerous thing.

In about 150 A.D., the Egyptian astronomer Ptolemy popularised Aristotle's vision by drawing a map of the world, complete with a big lumpy southern continent that he'd completely made up. Ptolemy, in putting pen to papyrus, had made *Terra Australis* real in the minds of future explorers.

In 1567, the Viceroy of Peru commissioned Álvaro

---

17   The new Catholics were generally unwilling to be discovered, but embraced their new religion when given the choice between kissing a cross and being nailed to it by a Spaniard.

de Mendaña to discover *Terra Australis*, find its gold, and convert its resident heathens. Australia narrowly avoided dancing to a flamenco beat when Mendaña rejected his navigator's proposed route, which would have intersected eastern Australia. Mendaña instead discovered the Solomon Islands, but failed to discover any new Catholics after offending the locals through his refusal to eat "a quarter of a boy with the arm and hand".

Mendaña returned to the Pacific in 1595. His trip inspired his young Portuguese pilot, Pedro Fernandes de Queirós, to mount an expedition. De Queirós was convinced *Terra Australis* existed and he was terrified that it would be discovered by the Muslims of the East Indies or the Protestant English, condemning the *Terra Australians* to an eternity of damnation. De Queirós believed he had been chosen by God to bring Catholicism to *Terra Australis* and hung about on Pope Clement VIII's doorstep making a nuisance of himself until the pope agreed to his mission.

De Queirós's two ships, both of which were named the *San Pedro*, set sail in 1605. The first few days were fun; everybody got drunk to celebrate the Feasts of Christmas, the Circumcision and the Epiphany. [18] But the good times soon stopped rolling.

The *Pedros*, the second of which was captained by Torres, carried a human cargo who would never have mixed

---

18   See footnote 8 for an explanation of Jesus's circumcision party. The Epiphany celebrates the coming of the Three Wise Men, irresponsibly bearing gifts of gold, frankincense and myrrh, all of which are choking or poison hazards for small children.

socially on the streets of Seville. The common sailors were forced to hang out with the useless nobility, most of whom were granted lucrative stipends for irrelevant jobs: there was the ship's poet, the cosmographer (there to explain the universe) and numerous would-be ambassadors for as yet undiscovered lands. The *entretenidos*, gentlemen of minor means, loafed around waiting for the expedition to find treasure. Then there were the lowest of the low, cabin boys kidnapped from Spanish beaches and slaves kidnapped from Africa. And finally, the Franciscan friars, who promised salvation to the heathen and damnation to any sailor tardy in fetching their slippers.

De Queirós enraged his sailors by putting them in irons for blasphemy and throwing their gaming tables overboard. He appalled the *Pedros*'s Spanish officers by being Portuguese. He antagonised the *entretenidos* by promising "as much silver and gold as you can carry and such quantity of pearls as you shall measure them by hatfuls" and delivering only coconuts. And he pissed off the Franciscans when he discovered *La Austrialia del Espiritu Santo*[19] (Vanuatu) and established a new crusading Order of the Holy Ghost to convert the natives – he made all the crew holy knights, including the two African cooks, and insisted that the Franciscans renounce their order for his.

De Queirós declared that he would build a new Jerusalem out of marble and gold on Vanuatu and claimed for

---

19   He named it Austrialia after Austria (as the Spanish royal family were the Hapsburgs of Austria), not, as is commonly recounted, Australia after *Terra Australis*. Australians still get upset when geographically challenged foreigners, usually Americans, mistake them for Austrians.

Philip III, Jesus Christ and the pope "all the islands and lands I have newly discovered, and desire to discover, as far as the South Pole". Other nations protested that it was unfair to claim land that you merely hoped to discover, but Spain used this new doctrine of aspirational discovery to justify its claim over the South Pacific for the next century.

De Queirós would tell anyone who listened that the tiny island he had found was the vast continent of *Terra Australis* (now *Cognita*). Torres, who had sailed around it, would quietly point out that this was nonsense. When Torres and de Queirós were separated by a storm after leaving Vanuatu, de Queirós, faced with a mutinous crew, barricaded himself in his cabin for three months and returned to the Americas. Torres continued the search for *Terra Australis* and came within a well-oiled whisker of landing at Cape York.

NEW HOLLAND WELCOMES CAREFUL SAILORS

By the end of the first decade of the seventeenth century, the world's spice trade was controlled by the *Vereenigde Oost-Indische Compagnie* (the Dutch East India Company), mercifully abbreviated to the VOC. The VOC was the first company in the world to issue shares and was almost a nation in itself, having been granted the power to form colonies, negotiate treaties, coin money and kill people for pepper.

On 26 February 1606, just months before Torres entered the Torres Strait, VOC captain Willem Janszoon landed the *Duyfken* near present-day Weipa on the Cape York Peninsula. He named the new land Nova Guinea and distinguished it from New Guinea, which he called Os Papua. To further complicate things, he named part of Os Papua Nieu Zelandt. Janszoon soon sailed home in a state of geographical confusion, but not before setting the template for many future contacts between Europeans and Aboriginal people.

While Janszoon's journals have been lost, VOC records refer to the "savage, cruel, black barbarians" he encountered. Unfortunately, it is not known what the Aborigines thought of the Dutch because they never had any journals to lose and nobody bothered to ask them, although their killing of nine of Janszoon's crew might offer some clue.

The Dutch, whether or not they started the violence, certainly knew how to dish it out. Jan Carstensz, who visited Cape York in 1623, testified that the Aborigines "have also knowledge of muskets whose terrible effects they have learned in 1606 from the men of the *Duiffken* who landed here."

Another Dutchman, Dirk Hartog, discovered Western Australia in 1616. He landed the *Eendracht* on a big island in Shark Bay, spent three days finding nothing of interest, nailed a pewter plate to a post and buggered off back to Batavia. His countryman Willem de Vlamingh visited the island eighty-one years later and took the Hartog Plate, replacing it with another plate (confusingly also known as the Hartog Plate). In 1801, the Frenchman Jacques Félix Emmanuel Hamelin came to see the famous plate and was

FIG. 1A: THE NATIVES OF THE SOUTH SEAS WERE
PERPLEXED BY THE DUTCH OBSESSION WITH PLATES ...

so moved that he left his own plate behind. Louis de Freycinet, a less culturally sensitive French tourist, stole the
second Hartog Plate in 1818.[20]

Australia's western shores were soon clogged with
Dutch seamen. Although VOC ships were ordered to turn
left before hitting New Holland, they kept bumping into
it because no one had worked out how to measure longitude at sea. And so the Dutch mapped much of western
and southern Australia over the following decades. The
first Dutch baby was born on Australian shores in 1626 and
several Dutch babies were murdered there in 1629 by the
psychopath Jeronimus Cornelisz.

20   You can see the first Hartog Plate in Amsterdam's Rijksmuseum and the
     second in the Western Australian Maritime Museum if you have nothing
     better to do than look at old plates.

Cornelisz, the pale and creepy second-in-command of the VOC trader *Batavia*, had planned to steal his ship's cargo and mutiny against Francisco Pelsaert, his schipper, but before he could carry out his evil plan the *Batavia* was wrecked on the Abrolhos Islands, off the western Australian coast. When Pelsaert set out for the East Indies in a longboat to arrange a rescue party, the survivors left behind made Cornelisz their leader. This is what is known in history as a Great Big Mistake.

Cornelisz believed his only chance of avoiding a mutiny trial was to kill any rescuers and make off in their ship with the *Batavia*'s salvaged cargo. For this he would need a band of loyal followers who would not give his plot away to the other survivors. It logically followed that there should be no other survivors to have the plot given away to.

FIG. 1B: ... BUT SOON CAME TO APPRECIATE THE CULTURAL DIFFERENCES BETWEEN DUTCH AND SPANISH EXPLORERS.

Before his eventual capture, Cornelisz successfully slaughtered over 120 men, women, children and babies in a bloody orgy that makes *Lord of the Flies* look like *Mary Poppins*. He had his hands cut off before being hanged from a makeshift gallows. His last words were "Revenge! Revenge!" (except in Dutch).

Several of Cornelisz's enforcers met a similar fate, but two were left on the mainland as Australia's first permanent European settlers. The children of local Aboriginal tribes are still sometimes born with blond hair.

After all this excitement, New Holland had something of a bad name with the Dutch. They still occasionally visited – Abel Tasman formally claimed Van Diemen's Land (now Tasmania) in 1642, a fact conveniently overlooked by British settlers a century and a half later – but they never stayed for long. Their attempts to sell pepper to the natives were met with confused smiles or rapidly hurled spears and there was no European market for sand or poisonous animals, the only things Australia seemed to produce in any abundance.

THE ONLY INTERESTING THING ABOUT WARRNAMBOOL

Some respectable historians contend that the Portuguese sailor Cristóvão de Mendonça explored the east coast of Australia in 1522 and that there are maps and a Portuguese shipwreck somewhere near the Victorian town of Warrnambool to prove it. Others call members of the Portuguese school nasty names and have stopped inviting them around for faculty nibblies. The people of Warrnambool are thrilled by all the fuss because it's the only time anyone has shown the remotest interest in them.

The Portuguese discovery theory goes something like this ...

Mendonça led a Portuguese fleet to eastern Australia but didn't tell anyone about it. However, we know he discovered Australia because in the mid-1500s some French guys from Dieppe copied Portuguese maps and drew something that looks awfully like eastern Australia, albeit if you've had a lot to drink and have never seen an atlas before. There's also a sixteenth-century Portuguese caravel made from mahogany down in Warrnambool and, although we can't remember where we put it, we're sure it will turn up soon.

The Dieppe maps were works of beauty intended for wealthy patrons – more art than science. French mapmakers were not overly concerned with accuracy and happily made up entire continents because they looked nice or because they couldn't draw any more ocean due to their blue pencil having gone missing. The Dieppe mapmakers regularly borrowed from folktales to make their maps more interesting. The Desceliers map of 1550 clearly labels where one might find fabulous one-breasted Russian warrior women and the legendary Prester John, an Ethiopian Christian king who had access to the Fountain of Youth and a magic mirror in which he could view any part of the world. [21]

Yet despite the unreliability of the Dieppe maps, some historians continue to pore over them. They alter the scale,

---

21   It is unknown how frequently Prester John used his magic mirror to spy on fabulous one-breasted Russian warrior women.

make adjustments based on assumptions about longitudinal error, rotate a quarter of the map ninety degrees, do some folding that would put a master origamist to shame, and then declare that the maps clearly depict the Warrnambool coast. Applying the same techniques, they could easily have reconfigured eastern Australia to look like Botswana or great-aunt Mabel's wooden leg.

As for the fabled Mahogany Ship, there have been no reported sightings since the 1880s and earlier accounts vary wildly as to the ship's location, size and construction. Two reputed pieces of the ship held by the National Library of Australia have since been identified as eucalyptus, a wood in scarce supply in sixteenth-century Portugal.

CHINESE SAILORS WITH NO JUNK

On 24 October 2003, President Hu Jintao of the People's Republic of China addressed a joint sitting of the Australian Parliament, opening with these words:

> Back in the 1420s, the expeditionary fleets of China's Ming Dynasty reached Australian shores. For centuries, the Chinese sailed across vast seas and settled in what they call the "southern land", or today's Australia. They brought Chinese culture here and lived harmoniously with the local people, contributing their proud share to Australia's economy, society and its thriving pluralistic culture.

President Hu's words were inspired by the international publishing sensation of 2002, Gavin Menzies' *1421: The Year*

China Discovered the World, which has been translated into twenty languages and sold well over a million copies.

Academics are, as a rule, bitter and twisted people who cope poorly when people without doctorates write bestsellers on their subject of expertise. Professor Felipe Fernández-Armesto of the University of London offers this view of *1421*:

> It is almost without exception wrong, factually wrong, and the conclusions drawn from it are logically fallacious, I mean, they are the drivel of a two-year-old. To say that it is devoid of evidence, logic, scholarship and sense was just about the nicest thing one could say about it. Because, I mean, you've got to be either a charlatan or a cretin, you've got to be either, you know, a kind of con man, or an innocent idiot in order to produce a book which is so lacking in any intelligence or accuracy whatever.

Fernández-Armesto disputes Menzies' thesis that in 1421, Zheng He, a giant Chinese eunuch who kept his dismembered member in a jewelled temple so that it might accompany him into the afterlife, led a fleet of over 100 aircraft-carrier-sized ships to explore every single continent, including Antarctica. Menzies contends that two of Zheng's equally genitally deficient admirals, Hong Bao and Zhou Man, split from the main fleet and separately discovered Australia's west and east coasts. Menzies writes:

> the most direct and persuasive evidence of the Chinese visits to Australia comes from Gympie … according to ancient Aboriginal tradition, a race of "culture heroes" sailed up this creek into Gympie's harbour in ships "shaped like birds".

He cites the eminent Australian historian Rex Gilroy, who discovered the "Gympie Pyramid" in 1975. Menzies is certain that Gilroy's pyramid was a Ming Dynasty observation platform, used by Zhou Man to monitor his extensive Queensland mining operations. He goes on to mount a uniquely compelling case that 90 per cent of Zhou's men died of radiation sickness after mining uranium in what is now Kakadu National Park.

Menzies relies heavily on Gilroy's groundbreaking work on early Chinese visits to Australia, which were first reported in a 1987 edition of *Australasian Post*, a publication well known for photographically charting the history of Australia's topless women and exclusive stories on men who have two penises or wear swarms of bees for beards. [22]

In just sixteen short years, a story published in a barbershop wank-mag, written by a conspiracy theorist who makes Oliver Stone and John Pilger look like Jemima Puddle-Duck and Mrs Tiggy-Winkle, would inspire the president of the People's Republic of China to claim centuries of Chinese settlement in Australia.

History is often like that.

THE MOST RIDICULOUS
DISCOVERY THEORY OF ALL

And amidst the buzzing static of the competing theories as to the discovery of Australia, you will hear whispers of

---

22 Gilroy's other articles for the *Post* include "Stonehenge Is Here" (February 1990), "Space Aliens in Australia" (September 1986), "Our Own Nessie" (May 1985) and the seminal "Why Yowies Are Fair Dinkum" (August 1980).

a heresy so outrageous, so manifestly absurd, so contrary to good sense and common decency, that it offends every notion of what it is to be Australian. It is the theory of the Unoriginal Non-Inhabitants.

2

The unoriginal
non-inhabitants

Yesterday upon the stair,
I met a man who wasn't there.
He wasn't there again today
I wish, I wish he'd go away.

Antigonish, William Hughes Mearns, 1899

THE PROBLEM OF ABORIGINAL HISTORY

I T IS DIFFICULT TO RECOUNT THE HISTORY OF a people who did not legally exist until the High Court of Australia said they did in 1992. The Court, in the *Mabo* case, shocked the nation with its findings that Australia had been occupied before British settlement and that the previously unknown inhabitants retained a legal interest in Australian land. [1]

---

[1]   Great Britain justified its claim of sovereignty over Australia on the grounds that it was "uninhabited waste and desert". The doctrine of *terra*

Apparently some black people had been hiding in our backyards for 60,000 years without ever having paid a day's rent and now they wanted to move into our houses with their tubercular dogs, spear dugongs in our swimming pools, ritually circumcise young boys in our garden sheds, and generally lower the tone of the neighbourhood.

These new Aboriginal and Torres Strait Islander people were a challenge to every right-thinking Australian, whether Angle, Saxon or Celt. But most of all, they were a challenge to historians. Innocent schoolchildren now needed to be taught to feel ashamed for being Australian and to say sorry for things they hadn't done. Heroic tales of the Anzacs, Ned Kelly and Shane Warne had to be replaced with boring stories about bunya nuts. Professors of Australian history were forced to accept essays handed in on bark, and to allow students to answer exam questions through the traditional mediums of painting lots of dots, banging two sticks together, or setting the examination hall on fire.

Australia's inconsiderate unoriginal non-inhabitants had also neglected to invent writing before the white man generously gave it to them. This meant the Aborigines only had a prehistory, rather than the proper history enjoyed by all civilised people. [2] Europeans gave Aboriginal people history. One would have expected just a little gratitude in return.

In 1993, the leader of the National Party of Australia, Tim Fischer, noted that the Aborigines had a stationary

---

nullius (literally land belonging to no one) meant Britain didn't have to pay compensation or apologise to anyone for settling Australia because there was nobody there to pay compensation or apologise to.

2   Aboriginal people claim they have an oral history, but this is just words.

culture that hadn't even invented the wheeled cart. Neither had they got around to inventing the horse or cow to pull it.[3] It was up to the white man to give these things to the Aborigines, along with the other trappings of Western civilisation like beads and mirrors, trousers and the treatments for smallpox and syphilis. It was even up to the white man to give the Aborigines smallpox and syphilis.

Did an Aborigine invent printing on the banks of the Rhine in 1440? Was Leonardo da Vinci a Pitjanjara? Did a Koori prevent World War III by inventing the atomic bomb? Let's face it, the Aborigines hadn't even thought of world war before white civilisation arrived in Australia. In 60,000 years, all the Aborigine managed to think up was a bit of bent wood that came back when he threw it. A smart man would have saved that time spent on research and development and simply trained a dingo to fetch it for him.

The fundamental problem with Aborigines is that they are lazy. The so-called "First Australians" simply couldn't be bothered to build the Pyramids, invade Poland, or bowl Mike Gatting around his legs with their first ball in an Ashes campaign. A proper history is built upon such great deeds. A proper history also requires lots of dates for things to have happened on. If there is no record of when things are done, then there can be no measure of progress. History is all about progress and Aborigines keep on getting in its way.

---

3   The Aborigines would no longer have been stationary had they invented the wheeled cart. Some argue that even if the Aborigines had invented the wheeled cart, they wouldn't have been able to train kangaroos to pull it. Rolf Harris conclusively proved that kangaroos are capable of pulling extremely heavy vehicles with his 1960 hit, "Six White Boomers". So it's good enough for Santa, but not good enough for Noel Pearson and his mates?

So, Aboriginal "history" reads something like this:

Abt. 58,000 B.C. (but we don't really know) [4]: Moved to Australia and failed to inhabit it.

Abt. 58,000 B.C. – Abt. 40,000 B.C.: Not much happened.

39,999 B.C.: Ate a big white grub that tasted a bit like chicken. [5]

39,999 B.C. – 1992 A.D.: "Wandered without certain habitation or proper laws" and "failed to exercise control of the land".

Abt. 12,000 B.C.: Did some finger painting on a cave wall. Ate another grub.

Abt. 11,999 B.C. – Abt. 2,001 B.C.: Mostly sunny with occasional showers.

Abt. 2,000 B.C. – 25 January 1788: Dingo introduced to Australia. Unexplained increase in missing baby reports.

26 January 1788 – present day: White man introduced to Australia. Explained increase in missing baby reports.

In the absence of written records, the only way to understand Aborigines and their past is to dig up their bones and give them to international museums. This enables historians to draw important conclusions about Aboriginal people. [6] However, "Aboriginal activists" have stopped this practice and have even demanded the return of these invaluable specimens so that they can blow smoke all over them and bury them where they were dug up from – which defeats the purpose of digging them up in the first place.

---

4   This just doesn't cut the historical mustard. The Aborigines would be far more interesting if we knew that they arrived in Australia just after lunch on 4 February 58, 572 B.C.

5   This is historical license, as the Aborigines had not yet invented the chicken.

6   For example, historians now know that the ancient Aborigines had bones.

The average Aborigine supports historians and mining companies in their large-scale excavation of Aboriginal burial sites, as this furthers humanity's knowledge of primitive Aboriginal lifestyles and provides the mineral royalties that furnish Aboriginal people with world-class health, education and passive welfare. The problem lies with the radicals, the troublemakers, the ones who have taken the benefits of our Western education and, without so much as a hint of thanks, flung it back in our faces by stirring up an issue where none existed for us before.

It is this lack of appreciation that hurts the most. Before white settlement, Aborigines were dying from toothache and skin infections; after white settlement, they were able to die from civilised diseases like measles and influenza. Before white settlement, Aborigines raised their children in primitive conditions; after white settlement, proper Christian families generously raised their children for them. Before white settlement, Aborigines lived in humpies deep in the outback; now they can live in humpies in some of the best outskirts of Brewarrina and Alice Springs.

In all of this, there is one word that best sums up the problem of Aboriginal history: Aboriginals.

THE PREHISTORY WARS

This is, of course, only one view of Aboriginal history. Before we consider alternative theories as to how Australia's unoriginal non-inhabitants didn't not come here and what they didn't not do after their failed non-arrival, we should talk a little about armbands.

FIG. 2: AN EARLY PORTRAIT OF A KANGAROO.

All Australian historians must wear either a black or white armband so that their views on Australian history and British settlers/invaders can be readily identified. Members of the Black Armband School believe that Australian history started about 60,000 years ago, that Aborigines have been left out of Australian history, and that the British invaders and their descendants have been giving Aborigines the rough end of the pineapple since 1788. They use words like "genocide", "Stolen Generations" and "sorry". They can also be identified by their beards and/or comfortable shoes and hybrid-car bumper-stickers that read "Kiss a Non-Smoker" or "It's Your ABC". Many members of this school are professional academics and handwringers.

Members of the White Armband School believe that Australian history started with Captain Cook in 1770 and that Aboriginal people, if they in fact exist, stumbled across Australia by accident, that nothing bad has happened to them since – but if it did, which it probably didn't, that was also an accident. They use words like "natural attrition", "vulnerable children in need of care and protection" and "Windschuttle". They can be identified by their rose-coloured glasses or their white-coloured canes and golden-coloured retrievers. Many members of this school work in talkback radio or conservative think-tanks.

AUSTRALIA'S FIRST BOAT PEOPLE

There is uncertainty as to when the first boat people bobbed their way to Australia, but most historians suggest that people started calling Australia home around 60,000 B.P.[7], give or take a few millennia.[8]

---

7   Before Peter Allen.

8   The oldest human remains found in Australia belong to Mungo Man and his much younger girlfriend (by about 14,000 years), Mungo Lady, both of whom

Australia was a very different place 60,000 years ago. It was so different that it wasn't even Australia, but a place called Sahul. Sahulians could walk from the Australian mainland to Tasmania or New Guinea without getting their feet wet because Australia was not nearly as girt as it is now. Sea levels were at least seventy metres lower and it would have been possible to paddle a bit of bamboo from the Asian mainland to Sahul without ever losing sight of land.

Most experts believe that Sahul was settled by a single group from whom all Aboriginal people are descended. Critics of this single-wave theory point out that there was enough bamboo in South-East Asia to build more than one raft, and if one group was able to make it to Australia, why couldn't two or three or forty-six?

Some Aborigines discount both the single-wave and multi-wave theories, believing instead that they were created in Australia through the forging of the elements with ancestral spirits.

Single-wave, multi-wave or no wave? This is one of the bloodiest battlegrounds of the Prehistory Wars.

NOBODY'S BITCH

Both single- and multi-wavers acknowledge that getting to Australia wasn't easy. The proto-Aborigines had to walk all

---

lived near Lake Mungo in south-west New South Wales. Mungo Man died about 40,000 years ago. His body was sprinkled with red ochre – the world's oldest example of ritual burial. Mungo Lady died about 26,000 years ago and her body was burned, smashed to bits, then burned again – the world's oldest example of being burned, smashed to bits, then burned again.

the way from Africa, putting up with tens of thousands of years of their children whining, "Are we there yet?" before they could start paddling their bamboo rafts.

Those on the long march through Asia would have clung to the coast, as the surrounding jungle was full of giant cats desperate to sample the new human-flavoured Whiskas. Man had lived his short life red in tooth and claw; eating and avoiding being eaten took up all of his energy and he simply had no time to compose a sonata for six sticks and hollow log, develop the iStone 2.0, or ask himself complex questions like "Why am I here?" [9]

Man finally discovered leisure while holidaying in Bali. One morning he woke up and saw some smoke from across the channel that separates Bali from the island of Lombok. Bali was getting a bit touristy, he thought – there were just too many people and tigers. So he unpacked his bamboo raft, which had been put away for a couple of millennia, and floated the thirty-five kilometres to Lombok. He had just crossed the Wallace Line, a deep ocean trench that forms a natural barrier between the ferocious beasts of mainland Asia and the soft and cuddly animals of Sahul.

Over in Lombok there was a 24-hour buffet of cute new animals demanding to be eaten. History shows what happens when man comes into contact with animals that have never met him before. The dodo of Mauritius was known for its inquisitive personality and its habit of sitting

---

9   This was actually a very easy question for early man to answer – "I am here because the ten-foot striped cat is not."

there while being clubbed to death by passing sailors. [10] The moa was a delicious twelve-foot-tall bird – the Maori thought it finger lickin' good and ate every single member of its eleven species within a couple of centuries of settling New Zealand. The miniature wombats of King Island moved into the "big warm burrows" of the sealers, who would let them trundle about their huts until they felt like another helping of wombat stew. Arthur Bowes, a First Fleet surgeon and one of the first men to encounter and eat Norfolk Island's enchanting bird life, summed up how man deals with animals that have not learnt to fear him:

> we had nothing more to do than stand still a minute or two & knock down as many as we pleas'd wt. a short stick – if you throwed at them and missed them, or even hit them with out killing them, they never made the least attempt to fly away & indeed they wd. only run a few yards from you & be as quiet and unconcerned as if nothing had happened.

In Lombok, man could eat his way through an entire island without running into anything bigger and nastier than himself. For the first time in history, man was nobody's bitch. This meant he could spend his new spare time working out how to stop his bamboo raft from sinking every few

---

10   The word dodo probably comes from the Dutch *dodaars*, meaning "fat arse" or "knot arse", a name gifted by Captain Willem van Westsanen in 1602. Other scholars suggest the name comes from the Dutch *dodoors*, meaning "sluggard", or the old Portuguese *doudo*, meaning "fool". The Dutch also referred to the dodo as the *walghvogel* or "loathsome bird". The dodo clearly had a major PR problem.

hours, telling campfire tales and painting pictures of all the animals he had just eaten. But just as culture was beginning to simmer in the saucepan of prehistory, the animals that were left wised up and the food ran out.

WHO KILLED SKIPPY'S MUM?

Man was hungry and hoped that the island on the horizon had not run out of obliging animals. So he pulled out his new improved bamboo raft and started paddling again. This pattern repeated itself until man ran into a really big island that would take a long time to eat out. That island was Australia.

The First Australians immediately noticed two things. First, there was no bamboo, so they wouldn't be returning to Asia to visit their stone-age in-laws. Second, the biggest, stupidest animal they had ever seen was sitting on the beach, thoughtfully stuffing nuts into its pouch, so that the Aborigines might celebrate their first Australia Day with a super-sized serving of *diprotodon à la bunya*.

The diprotodon was a marsupial. Marsupials didn't have to be smart because there were no really big warm-blooded predators in Australia. Australia also had the world's poorest soil, which produced plants low in nutrition and high in toxic chemicals. The low energy intake and high energy cost of breaking down poisonous plants meant marsupials had to conserve energy by shutting down their brains. [11]

---

11   Take the koala. The energy cost of breaking down eucalyptus oil means the koala can't do anything more strenuous than eat, sleep and piddle on Japanese tourists. The koala's evolution towards a smaller brain has been so rapid that its shrivelled cerebellum is too small for its skull, meaning it suffers

The skull of the diprotodon, the rhinoceros-like marsupial encountered by the First Australians, was filled with a tiny brain and enormous sinus cavities. The Aborigines would have been able to hunt down this gentle giant armed only with a pointed stick and a very large handkerchief.

The diprotodon was not the only example of Australian megafauna (Latin for "really big animal"). *Procoptodon goliah* was a ten-foot-tall kangaroo with a face like a gorilla, *Phascolonus gigas* was the original 200-kilogram wombat from hell, and *Genyornis newtoni* was an ostrich-sized duck. [12]

Professor Tim Flannery, one of Australia's best-known know-it-alls, supports the "blitzkrieg theory" of megafaunal extinction, the central tenet of which is: "The Aborigines did it." Flannery, who wears a Giant Extinct Kangaroo Armband, argues that the Aborigines rapidly spread across the continent, snacking on the biggest animals they could find as they went. The removal of all the giant herbivores about 47,000 years ago led to the rapid growth of thick underbrush, in which the increasingly nervous smaller animals were able to hide. The Aborigines solved this problem by torching the whole continent, destroying most of Australia's rainforests in the process.

Many Aboriginal people regard themselves as custodians of the land who have always lived in balance with nature.

---

concussion every time it turns its head. This is not actually a problem for the koala as it is too stoned on gum leaves to notice. Entire koala populations are now dying from chlamydia because koalas are too stupid to wear condoms.

12   *Genyornis* was a relative of Australia's extinct *Bullockornis planei*, affectionately known by palaeontologists as the Demon Duck of Doom on account of it being a quarter tonne, eight-foot-tall, kick-ass carnivorous duck.

They get a little tetchy when accused of megafaunal genocide and continental arson. Stephen Hagan, an Aboriginal
activist and academic, says:

> I would argue that Tim Flannery probably as a young kid had
> a very vivid imagination. He probably read a lot of fanciful
> British books as a young boy and he's grown up to be a little
> creative himself. There's no evidence of Aboriginal people liv-
> ing unsustainably. We live with our animals and the megafauna.
> I can't see if the megafauna were as big as they say they were,
> the size of two elephants ... it's going to take a lot of time for a
> tribe of thirty people to eat one elephant in a month let alone,
> as Tim Flannery said, eat them all out. I mean they would have
> had to bring all the 250 tribes, which was a million Aborigines
> in Australia before white man came. They would have had to
> bring all of them down to one tribal area to eat out all the ani-
> mals. I mean, how ridiculous is Tim Flannery?

Hagan and others who reject Flannery's death-by-
luncheon argument blame the weather. They say there is no
way people can munch through a whole continent before
the animals get suspicious and that fossil records show the
Aborigines and the megafauna frolicked happily together for
at least 10,000 years, until increased aridity resulting from
the last two ice ages caused the great megafaunal checkout.

THERE'S NO TIME LIKE DREAMTIME

Australian farmers whinge in cycles. When they're not
moaning about insufficient drought assistance, they're

demanding subsidised scuba gear for their cattle. This is because Australia doesn't have regular seasons like other continents. Instead it has El Niño and La Niña, which are Spanish for shitty weather.

The droughts and flooding rains caused by these *loco* weather systems meant that the Aborigines enjoyed years of plenty, interrupted by periods of wondering where all the food had gone. The times of scarcity kept populations low and required the Aborigines to forage widely for food. Living off the land was far easier than living on it, a fact that was lost on the British, who insisted that land could not be inhabited unless it was covered with castles, ornamental gardens and statues of inbred monarchs.

Nomads are not into possessions – it's hard to chase a kangaroo when you've got an ironbark dining suite with deluxe wombat-leather trimmings strapped to your back. So the Aborigines travelled light and invented tools that were specialised in design but generalised in application. A spear thrower might also be used as a water carrier, firestick, chisel, shield or musical instrument – the Aborigines conceived the Swiss Army Knife when the Swiss were still hiding in holes in the ground and smearing themselves with rancid bison fat.

While life was tough during the harsh times, food was abundant during the good years, so the Aborigines could spend a small part of their day doing boring hunting and gathering stuff and the rest of their time developing a complex and vibrant culture. Communities flourished and traded with each other, with shells from Cape York found as far afield as the West Australian coast. Over two hundred languages were whispered among the ghost gums, music was played under the stars, and the living rock and trees willingly gave up their flesh to the stain of hauntingly beautiful works of art. Animals were hunted, fish were fished and the rubbish was taken out to the midden every bin night. There was time for work, time for play, time for love and time for each other. Sure, there was also time for spearing people who looked at you a bit funny, but nobody's perfect.

The dingo arrived in Australia about 4,000 years ago, probably carried in the canoes of the Lapita, the ancestors of today's Polynesian people. The dingo was a tasty snack for long sea voyages – it was literally "dinner to go" and the Lapita were the world's first fast food delivery service. The Lapita were also the world's first great seafaring race[13] and carried their dingoes to Asia after their Australian stopover, as shown by kangaroo lice on Asian dogs. Dingoes roam the forests and plains of northern Thailand to this day. The dingo revolutionised Aboriginal society; it was hunting companion, pest exterminator and hot-water bottle rolled into one.

Through the lives of the hundreds of Aboriginal tribes that peopled Australia, with their different languages and customs, ran the common thread of the Dreamtime: a complex code for how life is to be lived, how food is to

---

13   The Lapita or their descendants may well have discovered the east coast of Australia when Captain Cook was nothing more than a gleam in the eye of his many-greats-grandmother. The Maori had legends of *Ulimaroa*, a vast land lying one month's hard paddling to New Zealand's north-west.

be gathered and how marriage, trade and disputes are to be regulated. It recognises that people are part of the land they inhabit and the land is part of the people.

The Dreamtime fuses past, present and future with the physical and spiritual worlds, leading Australia's greatest anthropologist, W.E.H. Stanner, to sum it up beautifully as "everywhen". James Bonwick, a nineteenth-century historian, said of the Aborigines, "they knew no past, they wanted no future".

Unfortunately for them, they got one on 26 January 1788.

Intermission

WELL, THAT'S THE ABORIGINES AND foreigners out of the way. Thank God for that. Now we can get back to some real Australian history: jolly convicts, villainous governors, rum, squatting with sheep, rum, gold diggers and other token women, geographically and nutritionally challenged explorers, rum, plucky Irish outlaws in scrap-metal couture, stump-jump ploughs and Coolgardie safes (stocked with rum).

But you've got time for a quick smoko before the good stuff starts, so light up a Winnie Blue, put a Bushells in the microwave and throw another Anzac biscuit on the Lazy Susan.

Ready? Then let's return to Captain Cook.

3

Rum, botany and the lash

... the females of most countries that
he has visited, have undergone
every critical inspection by him.

The Town and Country Magazine
on Joseph Banks, 1773

THE CAPTAIN AND THAT PLANT GUY

AUSTRALIANS KNOW ALL ABOUT CAPTAIN JAMES Cook. As schoolchildren, they dutifully traced his voyage from Plymouth to Australia in hand-me-down textbooks, made egg-carton and Paddle Pop-stick models of the *Endeavour*, and were dragged out in the rain to visit the uninspiring Captain Cook Monument at Botany Bay.[1]

Cook stares out at us from portraits, stamps and commemorative coins. The great captain stands tall and proud,

---

1   The monument honours Cook for first setting foot on Australian soil on 28 April 1770, although he didn't arrive until the following afternoon. There can be no finer tribute to Australia's "she'll be right" attitude than this error having remained uncorrected for over 140 years.

one hand resting on raised knee while the other proprietar-
ily fondles a sextant. He gazes into the middle distance, his
dour countenance that of a man confronted by the stench
of the ninety closely confined sailors whom he has recently
force-fed pickled cabbage in an attempt to ward off scurvy.[2]

Tourists can visit Cooktown in Queensland, board a
replica of Cook's ship in Sydney, or wonder why the hell a
1755 stone cottage owned by Cook's parents was transported from Yorkshire to Melbourne's Fitzroy Gardens.
Before leaving for home, they can purchase a Captain Cook
souvenir tea towel, a Captain Cook snowdome, or a Captain
Cook novelty apron with fake Captain Cook breasts.[3]

Cook is now considered the greatest navigator of his
era – the equal of Ferdinand Magellan, Vasco da Gama and
James Tiberius Kirk.[4] This would have surprised his peers,
as Cook only really captured the public imagination when
he became the meat between the bread in the Sandwich

---

2   Cook's men should have been grateful they didn't sail under Vitus Bering or
    Vasco da Gama. Vitus believed that scurvy could be cured by touching soil and
    perished from the disease and/or hypothermia shortly after being half-buried
    in the midwinter tundra of the island that now bears his name. Vasco insisted
    that his crew combat scurvy by gargling their own urine. Almost 70 per cent of
    his men died, leaving the survivors with a nasty taste in their mouths.

3   We know they are fake because Captain Cook's real breasts were barbecued
    by Hawaiians in 1779.

4   Captain James Kirk was named after Captain James Cook and the USS
    Enterprise was named after the HMS *Endeavour*. *Star Trek*'s catchphrase "to
    boldly go where no man has gone before" was inspired by Cook's journal
    entry "ambition leads me ... farther than any other man has been before
    me". *Enterprise* and *Endeavour*, the first and last space shuttles, were named
    after the ships of Kirk and Cook. There are bound to be other links between
    Captain Cook, *Star Trek* and the US Space Program and some Australian
    university will no doubt award a grant to explore this issue of undisputed
    national significance.

Islands (Hawaii). Before Cook was cooked, his greatest claim to fame was being the guy who steered the boat for the dashing Joseph Banks.

Most Australians vaguely remember Sir Joseph Banks as "that plant guy". Tourists intrigued by the great botanist must make do with visiting the Canberra suburb of Banks or Sydney's Bankstown. They are sadly unable to see Banks's reconstructed family home or buy Banks-themed kitsch.

This is terribly unfair because Banks was once known as "the Father of Australia". It was Banks who first recommended that the British establish a penal colony at Botany Bay. It was Banks who influenced early British thinking on relations with the Aboriginal people and advised the Crown on all matters New South Welsh during the first decades of settlement. It was Banks who instructed Matthew Flinders to circumnavigate Australia in order to put beyond doubt that it was a single continent. It was Banks who stole merinos from the Spanish, allowing generations of Australians to ride on the sheep's back. And it was Banks who got the mutiny-prone William Bligh into both breadfruit and governorship, indirectly contributing to the only military coup in Australian history. [5]

A normal man would have been exhausted by these great deeds, but Banks still had time to oversee British science for forty-one years, develop the Royal Botanic Gardens at

---

[5] Banks's role in shaping Australia was so neglected over the years that he wasn't recognised on an Australian stamp until 1970, and then he was only a background figure. Banks wasn't even the first botanist to be licked and stuffed into an Australian postbox, this honour falling to Sir Ferdinand Jakob Heinrich von Mueller in 1948 for his services to the macadamia nut.

Kew, organise voyages of exploration to Africa and Brazil, and engage in vigorous group sex.

So just who was Joseph Banks?

YOUNG MASTER BANKS

Joseph Banks came from a family of self-made lawyers and politicians whose vast piles of cash made the inbred aristocracy turn a blind eye to their vulgar origins.

At nine, Joseph was sent to Harrow public school[6] to learn Greek, Latin and archery (a compulsory subject until 1771). He was good at "organised games" but academically hopeless, so his father moved him to Eton at the age of thirteen.

Eton provided the finest education that money and selective breeding could buy. Its boys smoked pipes to improve their health and engaged in the quaint annual tradition of chasing a hamstrung ram before bludgeoning it to death with purpose-made ram bludgeoning clubs (more faint-hearted students could engage in school-sponsored badger, bull or bear baiting). With its rich assortment of terrified animals, Eton provided the perfect atmosphere in which Joseph's interest in natural history could flourish.

Banks moved on to Oxford despite his poor academic record and, like many young gentlemen of means, did not have to do anything so common as obtain a degree. University was a place for young men of breeding to mark

---

6   The English call their elite private schools public schools on the grounds
     that members of the public are allowed to attend in their capacity as butlers,
     porters, charladies and jolly red-faced cooks with tuckshop-lady arms.

time until they received their inheritances. Banks's father assisted by dying in 1761, leaving him estates yielding £6000 a year (Cook, in contrast, received £120 a year for commanding the *Endeavour*).

Banks spent his uni days studying plants and young women, with *The Town and Country Magazine*, a scandal sheet of unparalleled bitchiness, reporting, "Oxford echoed with his amours, and the bed-makers of _____ college have given the world some testimonials of his vigour ..."

Banks left Oxford in 1764 as a tall, unusually handsome and physically fit young man. He made friends easily, was successful with the ladies, and was richer than God. He was the type of man historians, who typically enjoy none of these characteristics, refer to as "a lucky bastard".

THE ENLIGHTENED BANKS

Banks was a devoted son of the Enlightenment, that era in European and American history when reason replaced blind faith, science replaced alchemy, and Sir Christopher Wren replaced Sir Isaac Newton's toilet roll every Tuesday afternoon because Sir Isaac was too busy inventing gravity.

The English Enlightenment began in 1687 with the release of Newton's *Philosophiae Naturalis Principia Mathematica*.[7] Newton and the other new scientists were devoted to personal observation and this inevitably led to self-experimentation. Newton once inserted a large needle into

---

7   The Australian Enlightenment began in 1988 with the release of John Farnham's *Age of Reason*.

his eye socket and rubbed it around "betwixt my eye and the bone as near to [the] backside of my eye as I could" because he was interested in the effect this would have on his vision (not good).

Henry Cavendish, the most brilliant physicist and chemist of the eighteenth century, sought to understand electricity by repeatedly exposing himself to increasingly powerful shocks, diligently describing the effects on his body until he lapsed into unconsciousness.[8]

William Stark, determined to unlock the secrets of scurvy, placed himself on a diet of bread and water until he contracted the disease. He then substituted the bread for one or two foods at a time in the hope he would find a dish that would perk him up a bit. Stark kept a daily diary of how sick he felt and died eight months into the experiment, while subsisting entirely on honey pudding and Cheshire cheese.

Banks shared the commitment of these great but incredibly stupid men to understanding the world through direct observation. As a teenager, he rubbed his face with toads to disprove the superstition that they caused warts. Banks applied this experimental spirit to natural history. He would not stay at home, waiting for the next shipment of exotic flora – he would bloody well go out into the world and pick some flowers.

---

8   Cavendish, now thought to have been an autistic savant, had only two
    interests: science and collecting period furniture. He was pathologically shy
    and would only communicate with his female servants by note: he added a
    staircase to the back of his mansion so he could run away whenever he heard
    his housekeeper approaching.

BANKS ABROAD

Young Englishmen of a certain class made the transition to manhood through a "Grand Tour" of southern Europe, visiting the art galleries and seedy bars of Paris and the grand cathedrals and bordellos of Rome. Grand Tourists were expected to collect things. Many collected ancient coins, Renaissance paintings or marble statues of ladies with wardrobe malfunctions. Nearly all collected interesting rashes. Upon their return, they would display their collections (except for the rashes) in glass cases or tasteful salons for their chinless friends to bray at.

Men of science were also collectors, but would study, sort and classify their acquisitions. Banks fell into this camp and, as others had already classified the plants of southern Europe, he determined to take his Grand Tour in Canada. The only way to get safely to Canada, recently surrendered by the French, was to hitch a ride with the Royal Navy. Banks had the connections to make this happen.

Banks had befriended his neighbour, John Montagu, the 4th Earl of Sandwich. Sandwich was a senior minister of the Crown and had recently been First Lord of the Admiralty, which meant he could get people on boats. Like Banks, he was interested in botany, fishing, drinking and prostitutes. Their "fishing trips" were legendary, with the philosopher David Hume reporting that they would pack "two or three Ladies of pleasure" to look after their rods and tackle. [9]

---

9   Sandwich was a notorious libertine and founding member of the Hellfire Club, which operated out of a converted abbey decorated with tasteful French pornography. Club members would attend dressed as monks or Biblical

Sandwich arranged for Banks to travel to Canada aboard the HMS *Niger*. Banks was in heaven. He studied jellyfish, killed a new kind of mouse, caught a 6 foot 11 inch halibut and collected numerous plants, animals and the scalp of Sam Frye, a fisherman who had been killed by Indians a year earlier, starting his lifelong fascination with collecting human heads. The return trip also led to Banks developing a lifelong prejudice against the Portuguese on the unusual grounds that "their Taste in Gardening is more trifling than Can be Conceiv'd".

But Banks's greatest success occurred in his absence. While he was murdering mice in Newfoundland, Sandwich had arranged for him to be elected a fellow of the Royal Society.

BANKS IN SOCIETY

The Royal Society was the premier British club for eggheads, carrying the very Enlightenment motto *Nullius in verba* (Take nobody's word for it). It included brilliant scientists, their wealthy patrons, and eccentrics like the Reverend William Borlase, who tabled regular papers on how much it was or wasn't raining in Cornwall. [10]

---

characters, get drunk and frolic with women dressed as nuns in luxuriously furnished caves under the abbey. Members liked to play pranks on each other. John Wilkes, the radical parliamentary reformer, once brought a baboon dressed in a cape and horns to a club function and convinced the inebriated Sandwich that it was the Devil. Sandwich, who never forgave Wilkes, later said to him, "Sir, I do not know whether you will die on the gallows or of the pox." Wilkes, one of the great wits of his age, immediately replied, "That depends, my lord, on whether I embrace your lordship's principles or your mistress."

10   Borlase's Royal Society paper, *An Account of the Late Mild Weather in Cornwall, of the Quantity Rain Fallen There in the Year 1762*, was only exceeded in

It was also a participant in the world's first international scientific venture: calculating the distance between the earth and sun by measuring the "transit of Venus" across the sun's face from various parts of the globe. Pairs of transits occurred eight years apart every 243 years and observations of the 1761 transit had been thwarted by war, bad weather and incompetence. The Royal Society decided it would send observers to Canada, South Africa and Tahiti for the 1769 transit.

Its choice to lead the Tahitian expedition was a middle-aged Royal Navy warrant officer who had just submitted a paper to the society titled *An Observation of an Eclipse of the Sun at the Island of New-Found-Land, August 5, 1766, by Mr. James Cook, with the Longitude of the Place of Observation Deduced from It.* Cook was the son of a farm labourer and a onetime grocer's apprentice who had started his sailing career hauling coal on the *Freelove,* one of Britain's more bohemian merchant vessels. He had killed some Frenchmen and drawn some nice maps of the Canadian coast during the Seven Years' War and was a keen astronomer to boot. Cook was promoted to the rank of lieutenant and told to pack his bags for Tahiti. He was also told to pack Joseph Banks.

Banks was not easy to pack. While the three Royal Society expeditions cost a combined £4,000, Banks insisted on carrying £10,000 worth of equipment. There was his

boringness by William Arderon's *An Account of Rain Fallen in a Foot-Square at Norwich.* Other Royal Society papers of the era included *An Account of the Degree of Cold Observed in Bedfordshire; Some Observations on Swarms of Gnats, Particularly One Seen at Oxford, August 20, 1766; Experiments and Observations upon a Blue Substance, Found in a Peat-Moss in Scotland;* and the gripping *Remarks on the Very Different Accounts That Have Been Given of the Fecundity of Fishes, with Fresh Observations on That Subject.*

natural history library, botanical trays and boxes, paints
and fine paper, numerous nets for snaring unsuspecting
fish, jars and alcohol for pickling insects, a sturdy boat,
and umbrellas for all weather conditions, ranging from fine
silk to heavy oilskin. Banks also took his botanical buddy,
Daniel Solander, a pudgy and humourless Swede; Her-
man Spöring Jr, a Finnish scientific dogsbody; the Scottish
artists Sydney Parkinson and Alexander Buchan; four servants; and two greyhounds. Space on board the *Endeavour*
was at a premium and the stoic Cook ended up sharing the
captain's cabin with Banks, Solander and an ever-increasing
number of plants and pickled animals.

Banks farewelled Harriet Blosset, his seventeen-year-
old fiancée, the night before he set sail. Banks, whose
feelings towards Harriet ranged between tepid and ambiv-
alent, did what any man would do when confronted with
an emotionally tricky situation. He got totally, utterly and
paralytically pissed.

BANKS IN TRANSIT

Banks spent his first days aboard the *Endeavour* empty-
ing his guts into the English Channel. His killer hangover
would not have seemed unusual to Cook's crew, who lived
on a steady diet of rum with occasional servings of sodomy
and the lash. The *Endeavour* had set sail with 604 gallons
of rum and four tons of beer. Alcohol was the first item
on the shopping list every time she pulled into port, with
3,032 gallons of wine picked up at her first stop at Madeira.
Each sailor was given a pint of 94 per cent proof rum a day,

except for the ship's boys, who had to make do with half a pint.

The *Endeavour*'s sailors were constantly tripping over each other, bumping into masts that shouldn't be there and pissing in Banks's seed trays. Robert Anderson, the ship's quartermaster, was flogged for extreme drunkenness when the *Endeavour* moored in Rio de Janeiro. John Reading, who was responsible for administering the flogging, was too sozzled to pick up the whip and was himself lashed. Reading later died of alcohol poisoning after drinking a pint and a half of rum in a single session, as did Robert Molyneaux, the ship's master. Dick Orton, Cook's clerk, got so spannered one night that a sailor was able to cut off his clothes and carve chunks from both his ears without waking him.

Life on board was hard. The *Endeavour*, which was only thirty-two metres long and nine metres wide, had to accommodate ninety-four men and two fictional children, [11] as well as dogs, cats, pigs, chickens and the ship's goat. Men lived in hammocks strung fourteen inches apart and were forced to wash their clothes in their own urine whenever fresh water ran low.

Cook had encountered problems getting decent kitchen help for the expedition. He rejected the first chef assigned to him for being too frail and was then given John Thompson, who had lost one of his arms below the elbow. Banks described the gastronomic delights served by the ship's short-hand cook:

---

11 Cook fraudulently registered his five- and six-year-old sons as crew to speed their eligibility to sit the Royal Navy lieutenant examination, which required previous service at sea.

Our bread indeed is but indifferent, occasioned by the quantity of Vermin that are in it, I have seen hundreds nay thousands shaken out of a single bisket. We in the Cabbin have however an easy remedy for this by baking it in an oven, not too hot, which makes them all walk off, but this cannot be allowd to the private people who must find the taste of these animals very disagreeable.

But Cook ran a better ship than most. The lash was used sparingly, principally on sailors who refused to eat their pickled cabbage. He demanded regular fumigation of the sleeping quarters and was so concerned about the hygiene risks posed by the defecating monkeys his sailors kept as pets that he had them all thrown shrieking into the Pacific Ocean.[12]

Banks enjoyed life at sea. He got to sleep in a comfy cabin and had packed lots of expensive wine and tasty treats for himself, but his greatest pleasure was sitting on deck and blasting passing seabirds out of the sky – his record was sixty-nine in a day.

The *Endeavour*'s stopover at Madeira gave Banks an opportunity to renew his prejudice against the Portuguese. He didn't like their people ("exceedingly idle, exceedingly conservative") or their wine ("ill made, ill cultivated, and carried on men's heads in goatskins") and amused himself by electrocuting Madeira's scientifically curious governor, giving "him as many shocks as he cared for; perhaps more".

The *Endeavour* crossed the equator on 25 October 1769, the first time Cook had ventured into the southern

---

12   The monkeys, not the sailors.

hemisphere. Cook was not a well-travelled seaman – even the ship's goat was more experienced, having circumnavigated the globe the previous year. Sailors, upon crossing the equator, would get absolutely plastered and dress up as the God of the Sea. Those who were crossing the line for the first time were dunked three times from the yardarm [13] unless they paid a fine in rum. Banks and Cook paid up.

The *Endeavour* stopped at Rio de Janeiro, where the viceroy – another despicable Portuguese – confined Cook and Banks to ship as spies because he could not believe that anyone would be stupid enough to sail around the world just to look at Venus or collect flowers. Banks risked his life by lowering himself out of his porthole in the middle of the night so that he could engage in a few hours' nocturnal botanising. [14]

He was finally able to venture ashore in daylight once the *Endeavour* had rounded Tierra del Fuego, where the Fuegian Indians received him "with many uncouth signs of friendship". Even the broadminded Banks was taken aback by the Fuegian custom of welcoming guests with a display of vigorous masturbation. [15]

---

13   Sailors found this an unpleasant experience, as the vast majority couldn't swim. Still, drowning was more pleasant than the eighteenth-century method of resuscitation. A drowning victim would awaken on deck to rudely discover his pants around his ankles, a tube inserted into his rear end, and some toothless deckhand vigorously blowing tobacco smoke up his khazi. The warmth of the smoke was believed to encourage respiration, but suspicion about the efficacy of tobacco enemas led to their disappearance by 1810 and the introduction of the popular expression "You're blowing smoke up my arse."

14   Banks first encountered the banana, which he loathed, in Rio. Banks and Dampier were generals on opposing sides of the Banana Wars, a fruity conflict largely ignored by historians.

15   Fuegian (trans): "We come in peace."

BANKS IN PARADISE

In Tahiti, Cook observed the transit of Venus, his men observed the topless Polynesian women in their grass skirts, and Banks observed the grass skirts, which were woven from a fascinating new subspecies of pili grass. Admittedly, he found it easier to study the skirts after gently prising the topless Polynesian women out of them.

Banks's account of his three months in Tahiti reads like a cross between *Gardening Monthly* and *Lady Chatterley's Lover*:

> In the island of Otaheite where Love is the Chief Occupation, the favourite, nay almost the Sole Luxury of the inhabitants; both the bodies and souls of the women are modeld into the utmost perfection for that soft science …

He continues breathlessly:

> The foremost of the women … quickly unveiling all her charms gave me a most convenient opportunity of admiring them by turning herself gradually round … she then once more displayd her naked beauties and immediately marchd up to me … I took her by the hand and led her to the tents accompanied by another woman her friend, to both of them I made presents but could not prevail upon them to stay more than an hour.

But Banks was not solely interested in sex and botany. He learned the Tahitian language, was intrigued by the Tahitians' tattoos (Banks introduced the word "tattoo" into the English language), wanted to take up surfing after seeing the locals ride the waves, and participated in a religious ceremony wearing only a loincloth and body paint.

Cook's time in paradise was less pleasant. Repairs to the *Endeavour* were seriously threatened when the crew stole 120 pounds of nails, which were the Tahitian currency for negotiable affection. Cook's relations with the locals grew increasingly strained as a result of their tendency to make off with anything that wasn't nailed down (which was quite a lot following the disappearance of the nails). The instrument necessary to measure the transit disappeared within twenty-four hours of being brought ashore and, although the athletic Banks recovered it after chasing the thief for seven miles, Cook, the drunken astronomer Green and Solander all recorded different times for the transit. The mission was an astronomical failure.

By the time the *Endeavour* set sail, Banks had convinced two locals, Tupia and Tiata, to return to England with him. He wrote of Tupia:

> I do not know why I may not keep him as a curiosity, as well as
> some of my neighbours do lions and tygers at a larger expence
> than he will probably ever put me to ...

BANKS DOWN UNDER

Although Cook had secret orders to sail south from Tahiti to find *Terra Australis*, he considered the search for an imaginary continent to be a complete waste of time. After discovering lots of empty ocean he sailed to New Zealand, which Banks, despite all evidence to the contrary, insisted must be the mythical Great Southern Land.

While the Maori spoke Polynesian, they were nothing like the Tahitians, being more interested in eating Cook's crew than giving them a full-body breadfruit massage. Cook

Fig.3: Joseph Banks and his assistants collected Australian natives for the royal nursery at Kew.

believed he could "cultivate a friendship with the natives" by
kidnapping them and then being kind to them. He found
it hard to get to the being kind part, however, as the Maori
showed their displeasure at being kidnapped by fighting to
the death. After four Maori were killed by Cook's kindness,
Banks recorded, "Thus ended the most disagreeable day my
life has yet seen that such may never return to embitter my
reflections." However, he perked up a few days later when
one of the local cannibals gave him a human head for his
collection.

After charting New Zealand, Cook decided to head
home via the "East coast of New Holland" and, on 19 April
1770, sighted Australia. Banks was unimpressed. He wrote
that the land reminded him of "the back of a lean Cow"
and was "in every respect the most barren countrey I have
seen", but he was happier than Larry when the *Endeavour*
moored at Sting Ray Harbour. Cook was so struck by the
image of the insanely grinning Banks emerging from the
undergrowth with novel plant life strapped to every square
inch of his body that he renamed the harbour Botany Bay.

The Gweagal of Botany Bay initially ignored the
Endeavour and its crew of white ghosts but, when Cook
made for shore, two warriors pelted the landing party with
stones and spears. Cook responded with gunfire, wound-
ing one and forcing both to flee. All attempts at further
contact were rebuffed, with Cook wistfully reporting that
"all they seem'd to want was for us to be gone".

The *Endeavour* sailed up the coast, occasionally setting
Banks ashore to pick flowers and terrorise the local wildlife. Banks named the kangaroo and quoll, adopting the

local Aboriginal names, and described the dingo, a species of possum and the flying fox, which one superstitious sailor believed to be the Devil. [16]

Cook, belying his subsequent reputation as a master mariner, then ran the *Endeavour* straight up the guts of the Great Barrier Reef, a structure that can be seen from outer space, but apparently not from one hundred yards. The local Aborigines were reserved, but displayed some signs of friendliness when they were not trying to burn Cook's camp to the ground. [17] Banks spent a happy seven weeks botanising while the ship was repaired. He even had an opportunity to test his theory that the natives were just Polynesians in need of a good bath by rubbing an Aborigine's skin with spit. Banks only conceded that the Aborigines were a distinct people when this attempt to relieve the unfortunate native of his "exceeding blackness" failed.

The *Endeavour* finally limped away from the Queensland coast and reached Possession Island in the Torres Strait on 22 August 1770, where Cook claimed eastern Australia for Great Britain. His orders from the Admiralty concerning *Terra Australis* instructed, "You are also, with the consent of the natives, to take possession of convenient

---

16   From this, one might infer that Satan is small, furry and hangs upside down in trees eating fruit. But sailors' descriptions of wildlife are not to be trusted – sailors also mistook the dugong, which is the world's ugliest animal, for a gorgeous bare-breasted lady with the tail of a fish, giving rise to the legend of the mermaid.

17   Firestick farming is not just useful for clearing the land of undergrowth. It's also great for clearing the land of uninvited white people. Aboriginal warriors frequently used fire as a weapon in their conflicts with the British invaders. The Aboriginal tendency to torch anything vaguely flammable led Cook to describe Australia as "this continent of smoke".

situations in the country in the name of the King of Great Britain."

Cook's views on the niceties of this dispossession would have been influenced by Banks, who was scathing in his assessment of the locals. He labelled them "the most uncivilizd savages perhaps in the world" and "rank cowards" because of their habit of running away from men who wanted to shoot them or rub them with spit. They were "ignorant of the arts of cultivation", wandered "like the Arabs from place to place" and, he concluded from their indifference to the beads and other old tat generously proffered by Cook, had no interest in property. Banks believed that the Aborigines thinly populated the coast and, having apparently dozed off during logic classes at Oxford, he posited:

1. Aborigines only eat seafood.
2. There is no seafood inland.
3. Therefore there are no Aborigines inland.

Banks's view that the vast interior of New Holland was empty and its coasts sparsely populated by a handful of homeless savages who wouldn't even ask King George for his beads was hugely influential on later British policy.

BANKS TAKES TO BED

After casually pocketing half a continent, Cook sailed with all haste to Batavia, the nearest European-controlled port. Batavia was built by the Dutch, who love canals, and the city's marble-lined waterways eased their homesickness.

But those same waterways trickled liquid death – because the only living things in all God's creation that love canals more than the Dutch are mosquitoes. Batavia was a malarial Mecca and its bloodthirsty pilgrims launched an airborne jihad against the *Endeavour*.

Cook's entire company, with the exception of John Ravenhill, sunk into fevered delirium. Ravenhill, the *Endeavour*'s oldest sailor at almost eighty, was noted for being "generally more or less drunk every day". The crew concluded that hard liquor was the secret to his health and exacerbated the crisis by drinking vast quantities of rum. [18] William Monkhouse, the ship's doctor, was the first to die. Six others followed, including Tupia and Tiata, depriving Banks of the opportunity to display them as curiosities at London dinner parties.

Banks determined that if he was to ascend the Final Trellis to the Great Arboretum In The Sky, then he would do so in comfort. He set himself up in a luxurious villa, where his convalescence was aided by eight slaves and two obliging Malay women. Recovered, he rejoined the *Endeavour* as it crawled out of Batavia. Forty of the crew were still incapable of leaving their hammocks and fever and dysentery stalked the ship all the way to Cape Town. Thirty-four men were lost by the time she made port, including Parkinson, Spöring and the astronomer, Green, who died from hanging his legs out of a porthole in a suspected

---

18   They would have been right had they drunk vast quantities of gin and tonic, as the quinine in tonic water was the world's first effective anti-malarial. Unfortunately the gin and tonic was not invented until 1825.

rum-fuelled "phrenzy".[19] Then, to the surprise of everyone, John Ravenhill's lifeless body was found one morning, embalmed in enough rum to open a small bar. Drinking levels suddenly dropped.

Banks now turned his eyes towards home. He could not have imagined, even in his most fevered malarial dreams, the reception he would receive upon his return.

THE IMMORTAL BANKS

Joseph Banks was a publicity slut. As soon as he stepped off the boat, he let the world know that he had singlehandedly discovered around 1,400 plants and over 1,000 animals. He took to the podium at Oxford and Cambridge, where staid men of science screamed hysterically and hurled their long johns at him. Carl Linnaeus, the father of modern botany and taxonomy, dubbed him "the immortal Banks" and lobbied for New South Wales to be renamed Banksia.

The reptiles of Fleet Street crawled out from under their paving stones to bask in the sunlight that beamed from Banks's backside, scribbling grovelling homages while reminding their readers that Cook was a mere lieutenant. Banks was a must-have guest at all the right parties and became a confidante and frequent companion of King George III (it is not surprising that Mad King George formed an attachment to the dashing young botanist, given his later penchant for talking to trees).

---

19 This is one of history's more confusing causes of death. It is not clear whether Green's drunken legs caught a chill, were crushed between the ship's hull and an iceberg, or were ripped off by a passing shark.

Nor were women immune to Banks's charms. Having quietly paid Miss Blossett £5,000 to go away, Banks became the patron of a young lady who had been left penniless when her father died under the weight of his gambling debts. He provided her with a comfortable house and an illegitimate daughter, the only child he would ever have. Banks also entered into a relationship with his housekeeper, who became his well-known-but-socially-invisible-in-polite-company mistress. *The Town and Country Magazine* salaciously reported these extra-botanical activities.

The other great celebrity to emerge from the voyage was the *Endeavour*'s goat, which was awarded a silver collar engraved with a poem penned by Dr Samuel Johnson (of dictionary fame) for the occasion:

In fame scarce second to the nurse of Jove,
This goat, who twice the world had traversed around
Deserving both her master's care and love,
Ease and perpetual pasture now has found.

Cook's reception was not so happy. He returned home to find that his two youngest children had died and was given such a bollocking by the Royal Society for the inconsistent measurements of the transit that the terms of his censure were excised from the society's official proceedings. The public regarded him as Banks's flunky and he remained very much a B-grader on the tea and cucumber sandwiches circuit.

Banks now lobbied Sandwich, who had been reappointed First Lord of the Admiralty, to give him two ships to mount a final search for *Terra Australis Incognita* and insisted that Cook command them. Within a month of the *Endeavour*'s return, Cook found himself again ordered to search for a continent he believed he had already proved didn't exist.

The *Resolution*, Cook's flagship, was bigger than the *Endeavour* but not big enough for Banks, who demanded that he and his now significantly extended entourage be given the captain's cabin and that the whole deck be raised a foot to give him extra headroom. The completion of these modifications was hampered by the on-board parties Banks threw for his groupies. When they were finally complete, the changes so overbalanced the ship that Cook refused to put her to sea and Sandwich ordered that the ship be restored to her original state. John Elliott, a midshipman on the *Resolution*, recounted Banks's response:

> ... when he saw the Ship, and the Alterations that were made, He swore & stamp'd upon the Wharf, like a Mad Man; and instantly order'd his Servants, and all his things out the Ship.

Banks withdrew from the expedition in a huff. His resignation was so sudden that one of his entourage, Mr Burnett, did not hear the news and travelled as planned to meet the *Resolution* at Madeira. Cook wrote to the Admiralty, "Every part of Mr Burnett's behaviour and every action tended to prove that he was a Woman." Banks had apparently been taking mistress-smuggling tips from the French.

When Cook returned and was feted for (again) disproving the existence of *Terra Australis*, Banks sulked.

However, the pair were reconciled after Cook gave Banks a new Tahitian, Omai.

Cook attributed the loss of only one sailor to illness during the three-year voyage to his making his men get out of their wet clothes, stay out of draughts, clean their hammocks, eat their greens, drink plenty of fluids and wash up after every meal. While this makes perfect sense to every parent of a teenage boy, these were revolutionary concepts for the Royal Navy. The Royal Society was so impressed with Cook's ideas for not killing his crew that it awarded him the 1776 Copley Medal for being the year's biggest pointy-head.

In 1776, Cook set out for his fateful third voyage. Officially, his mission was to return Omai to Tahiti. This seemed an awful lot of effort for one Tahitian: the voyage's true purpose was to discover the fabled North West Passage, thought to connect the Pacific and Atlantic Oceans. During the voyage, Cook displayed unprecedented cruelty, refusing rations to sailors who could not bring themselves to eat walrus and ordering the ship's barber to cut off the ears of a native suspected of theft. He fell into cold rages, behaved autocratically and suffered periods of listlessness. Some scientists now attribute these personality changes to a dietary deficiency caused by intestinal worms. Others say he was just in a shitty mood.

It all went horribly wrong in Hawaii. Cook was wrapped in red cloth, stuck atop a rickety scaffold and given a pig by a bunch of Hawaiians who thought he was their god Lono. Cook did not get to enjoy his divinity for long, as his worshippers soon stabbed him, cut him into small pieces and roasted him, before thoughtfully offering a fillet of Cook to his horrified crew. The manner of Cook's death, rather than his achievements in life, finally made him a pin-up in Britain.

Banks had not been idle during Cook's absence. He had spent several productive years doing what he did best: schmoozing. In 1778, he was elected secretary of the Dilettante Society, which sponsored the study of Greek and Roman art but was condemned by its critics as "a club, for which the nominal qualification is having been in Italy, and the real one, being drunk".

It was electricity, however, that gave Banks his biggest break.

Benjamin Franklin had made his name by tying a metal key to a kite and flying it in a storm, thereby proving that lightning was electricity. This led to his invention of the lightning rod, which stopped tall buildings and ships from regularly exploding and earned Franklin an invitation to join the Royal Society, even though he was an American.

When Franklin helped to draft the US Declaration of Independence, his American-ness became a problem. His spiked lightning conductors were declared unpatriotic by King George III, who pressured the president of the Royal Society, Sir John Pringle, to endorse an ineffective British alternative that used a knob instead of a spike. Pringle refused, explaining, "Sire, I cannot reverse the laws and operation of Nature," and the Royal Society was soon looking for a new president.

Although he was only thirty-five and had not written a single scientific paper, Banks was elected as the society's president because of his royal connections and his belief that pragmatism trumped the laws and operation of Nature every time.

It was now time for Banks to attain full respectability. He married a woman with a pedigree and a large bank balance and devoted his time to socialising and politicking over long lunches, rapidly expanding both his influence and his trouser size. He was now one of the most powerful men in the British Empire. And he had plans for New South Wales.

4

On our selection

My object all sublime
I shall achieve in time
To let the punishment fit the crime
The punishment fit the crime

The Mikado,
W.S. Gilbert, 1885

THE TROUBLE WITH TEA

AUSTRALIA, AS ITS MOST VICIOUSLY ELOQUENT prime minister, Paul Keating, once pointed out, "is the arse end of the world". So what inspired Great Britain to select distant Botany Bay as the outhouse of its empire?

Let's start with tea.

The English love tea. So do Americans. That's because for most of the eighteenth century Americans were just a subspecies of Englishman who talked big, ate a lot of turkey and wore dead racoons on their heads. The Americans loved tea so much that they stopped loving the English because the English kept taxing American tea consumption.

In 1698, the British East India Company had been granted a monopoly to bring tea into Britain, enabling it to charge exorbitantly for its product. The British government, determined to take its cut, imposed a 25 per cent import duty, further inflating tea prices. In 1721, the British Parliament passed a law requiring its American colonies to buy tea exclusively from Britain. The company sold its tea to English dealers, who on-sold it to desperate American pot and spout addicts, passing on the duty and engaging in further price gouging.[1]

Things got even worse after the Seven Years' War ended in 1763. The British left a standing army in America and, unwilling to raise taxes at home to pay their soldiers, taxed the Americans for the first time. In 1767, the Chancellor of the Exchequer, Charles Townshend, introduced the *Townshend Acts* to tax tea in the American colonies. This followed the 1764 *Sugar Act* and 1765 *Stamp Act*, which taxed the sugar needed to sweeten tea and the paper needed to make teabags. The only untaxed part of the tea supply chain was the little string that always breaks just when you need to remove the teabag from the cup. The Americans knew it was only a matter of time before the British hit them with the *Defective String Act*.

The Americans were no longer prepared to lie back and think of England; they were going to stand up and shout a lot in their big loud American voices. They flocked to join the Sons of Liberty, vigilantes who beat up importers of British goods and put mountain lions in tax collectors' beds.

---

[1]   The dealers maximised their profits by lowering the purity of tea by cutting it with hot water and milk. Earl Grey, the kingpin of a notorious tea cartel, later diluted the product further by adulterating it with bergamot.

They also boycotted British tea and promoted alternatives like Labrador tea, brewed from Canadian rhododendrons. Unfortunately Labrador tea contained ledol, a potent toxin that caused severe stomach cramps and paralysis. This made some Americans desperate enough to switch to coffee.[2]

Things reached crisis point in 1770, when a Boston wig-maker's apprentice accused an English soldier of not paying for a wig.[3] A mob assembled to demand the return of the wig and the soldiers responded with musket fire, killing five men. The soldiers were defended by John Adams, who secured their acquittal by arguing that the Bostonians were "a motley rabble of saucy boys, negroes, and molattoes, Irish teagues and outlandish jack tars". Adams would go on to lead the motley rabble as the second president of the United States.

The American kettle really started boiling with the passage of the 1773 *Tea Act*, which removed British tea duties and allowed the British East India Company to deal directly with American dealers. Although this made tea cheaper, the Americans were outraged that the Townshend tax was maintained.

---

2   American coffee is the worst drink in the universe. The Indonesians make a coffee, known as *kopi luwak*, from beans that have been squeezed through the anus of a wild Asian palm civet. Luwak is much, much better than the insipid, tepid, overly sweet coffee favoured by Americans, which tastes like it has been drained from the bladder of a diabetic skunk.

3   An eighteenth-century Englishman's social standing could be inferred from the styling and size of his wig (hence the term "bigwig"). The wig craze reached its apogee in the 1780s, with the introduction of eyebrow wigs made from mouse skin. A good wig cost about twice a common labourer's annual wage (eyebrow wigs were cheaper) and wigs were commonly targeted by thieves to sell on the thriving wig black market. Not paying for a wig was a big deal.

In December 1773, four Company ships travelled to Boston, while others made for New York, Philadelphia and Charleston. The Sons of Liberty successfully pressured most of the captains to return their cargoes to Britain, but the lieutenant governor of Massachusetts, Thomas Hutchinson, had a vested interest in unloading tea in Boston: his family had secured the right to sell it. Hutchinson prevented the captains from leaving port with their cargo and the citizens of Boston prevented them from unloading. The Bostonians resolved the impasse by throwing a Tea Party. They stormed the ship, many of them poorly disguised as tea-hating Mohawk Indians, and threw all 342 crates of tea into Boston Harbor,[4] turning it into a giant, albeit cold and salty, cup of Lapsang souchong.

The British attempted to close Boston port until the Bostonians paid for the destroyed tea and said they were sorry. The Bostonians told the rest of America how mean the British were. Within two years the Americans were revolting.

The Revolutionary War meant that the Americans refused to import the convicts that Britain had been dumping on them since 1718. Britain desperately needed somewhere new to store all its poachers, rapists and Irishmen.

THE BLOODY CODE

Britain's inability to export its convicts was a major problem. An Englishman couldn't walk out his front door without tripping over a criminal, as it was almost impossible

---

4   This was the world's first bottom of the harbour tax avoidance scheme.

for a person not to commit three capital offences before breakfast.

Before 1688, about fifty crimes were punishable by death, but the ever-increasing gap between what the haves had and the have-nots hadn't led to a proliferation of laws designed to protect property. By 1815, 215 crimes could score you a date with the hangman, earning the British criminal law its "Bloody Code" moniker. The noose awaited those convicted of removing a rabbit from its warren, interfering with a fishpond, having a blackened face, or being in the company of gypsies for a month.

The Code was riddled with anomalies. Sheep thieves were hanged while goat thieves were treated with kid gloves. Stealing cloth was a capital felony, while "Stealing and selling negroes, the property of others" was a mere misdemeanour. Pickpocketing carried the death penalty, but child stealing did not (unless the child was stolen from a very large pocket). In 1772, a man who sexually assaulted his young niece was given a few lashes of the whip along-side a man who had stolen a radish. [5] Murder could only be proven if malice aforethought was established, so murderers were often charged with some lesser but easier to prove capital offence – for example, a servant who hit his master fifteen times with an axe was hanged for entering his master's study without permission.

---

5 Crimes against children were only severely punished if they had real novelty value, as in the case of the sheep farmer who pretended to take bastard boys in as apprentices, only to castrate them and sell them to the local opera company.

COUNTRY MATTERS

The Code was also designed to keep country people in their place – face down in the muck under the boot heels of wealthy landholders. The 1671 *Game Act* imposed the death penalty on those who hunted hare, partridge, pheasant or moorfowl, even on their own land, unless they had large estates or were closely related to someone who did. The propertied rich could hunt wherever they liked and were perfectly entitled to enter a peasant's smallholding and trample his turnip crop in pursuit of a pheasant.

The game laws were later extended to hunting deer and other edible animals on land without the owner's permission. [6] The lower classes, who had hunted on local estates for centuries, considered these laws unfair and would sneak onto their betters' property at night, with faces blackened to prevent identification. This led to the introduction of the hated 1723 *Black Act*, which made it a capital offence to have a face blacked or otherwise disguised, striking terror into the heart of every coalminer, [7] chimneysweep and politically incorrect minstrel.

The *Enclosure Acts* required properties to be fenced, which was expensive and prevented the poor from grazing their livestock on common land. Small landholders were

---

6　Eating humble pie, made from a deer's entrails or "humbles", became a status symbol – the term now has the opposite meaning to its Georgian usage.

7　The Act was once used to prosecute coalminers who vandalised a tollbooth. The prosecutor couldn't prove which miners did the vandalising, so prosecuted them all for having black faces. Legal scholars pointed out that the Act doubly discriminated against coalminers as they could also have been prosecuted had they washed their faces, as clean coalminers would be regarded as going about disguised.

forced to sell up and work the ever-expanding estates of the gentry or try their luck in the city.

Poaching was not the only capital crime routinely committed by country folk. England had a population of eight million people in the late eighteenth century and about 20,000 of them were smugglers. Tea was the smuggler's contraband of choice, with an estimated 21 million pounds of the beverage smuggled into England in 1783.

The Bloody Code was also used to prosecute wreckers, sinister Cornish folk who specialised in dampening lighthouse fires and luring vessels onto the rocks with cheerily waved lanterns. The law allowed salvagers to keep goods recovered from shipwrecks – as long as there were no survivors. Those lucky shipwreck victims who lasted through the night by clinging to a bit of driftwood were greeted by the silver light of dawn – and determined-looking Cornishmen with pitchforks wading towards them.

The most glamorous villains of the English countryside were highwaymen – commonly well-bred and literate young gentlemen who lacked an inheritance.[8] One highwayman letterboxed a wealthy London suburb, politely warning its residents not to leave home without at least ten pounds and a watch if they wished to avoid being shot when held up.

These rakes of the road often considered it poor form to rob women and were exceedingly image-conscious. John Rann, known as "Sixteen-string Jack" for the sixteen

---

8   There were also a few highwaywomen, including the 1.37 metre tall Elizabeth Ford, the only highwayperson known to hold up stagecoaches on a Shetland pony.

multicoloured silk strings tied to the knees of his elegantly tailored breeches, went to the gallows in 1774 wearing a specially commissioned green suit, a giant nosegay and a hat covered with silver rings. James MacLaine was a handsome clergyman's son who terrorised the roads north of London so that he could afford to host society dinners. After being sentenced to hang, he received 3,000 visitors in his cell in a single day, most of them well dressed and tearful young women.

The changes that swept the British countryside during the eighteenth century, and the persecution of honest folk who engaged in traditional rural pastimes such as hunting partridges and shipwreck survivors, resulted in a mass migration to the cities. And one city's siren call could be heard above all others.

BABYLON ON THE THAMES

Refugees from the countryside found themselves in the kaleidoscopic hubbub that was London, with its jumbled alleys and open sewers; its marble palaces and unmade hovels; its shuffling beggars and sad-eyed turnspit dogs;[9] its priests, politicians and panderers. Every vice ever

---

9   Every inn had a spit-roast. Innkeepers found that servants assigned to turning a spit for hours would wander off to do something more interesting. So they bred "long-bodied, crooked-legged and ugly dogs" to run in a wheel suspended above the fireplace, which would turn the spit. Everyone was pleased with this arrangement, except for the turnspit dogs, which not surprisingly were described as having "a suspicious, unhappy look about them". The unpleasant nature of the work meant the dogs worked in shifts, which may have given rise to the proverb "Every dog has its day." Turnspit dogs, as an added indignity, were also taken to church as foot warmers. The breed mercifully became extinct after the invention of the steam-powered rotisserie.

conceived nested in the dark corners of this city – a city where little was valued, but everything was negotiable.

Londoners sought solace from these surroundings in gin. In 1750, one in every fifteen houses in the City of London was a pub. In Westminster, in London's West End, it was one in eight, and in the neighbouring parish of St Giles, one in four. Scurvy rode through the winter streets on its pale horse, while summer served up a smorgasbord of fatal poxes and fevers. The children of the poor were expected to start work by the age of four; they could be found begging, combing the city for dog shit (which, along with cat's brains and human urine, was used to tan leather) or being stuffed up chimneys.

By the mid-eighteenth century, London had a population of 650,000 people, of whom a staggering 62,000 are estimated to have engaged in prostitution. [10] Women generally could not own property, and their work options were limited: they might take jobs as poorly paid servants or as seamstresses. Prostitutes euphemistically gave their occupation as "seamstress" when arrested, which greatly upset the genuine seamstresses who constantly had to ask furtive-looking men to stop hanging around their dress shops.

While London housed great poverty, it was also home to great wealth. Gradually, it dawned on the poor that they were missing out on something. The poor were assaulted by the sight of the well-to-do walking the streets in their fine silks, holding tea-parties on the bank of the Thames,

---

10 Not all eighteenth-century prostitutes were women. A 1780s raid on Covent Garden, London's red lamp capital, netted twenty-two ladies of the night, two of whom were men dressed in drag.

and laughing gaily as they stuffed vast quantities of tobacco up their nostrils. [11]

London's aspirational poor were ingenious at devising new ways of parting people from their property. Tom Gerrard taught his dog to pick pockets and was eventually hanged as an accessory to the dog's crimes. Roderick Audrey, a sweet-faced boy, trained his pet sparrow to enter London townhouses. He would knock on the door, bottom lip trembling, and beg the butler to let him in to retrieve his beloved pet. Once inside, he would grab the bird and as much gilded cutlery as he could stuff down his trousers. Obadiah Lemon would cast a hooked line into the windows of passing coaches, depriving passengers of their hats, wigs, scarves and the occasional eye.

But London's greatest criminal genius was undoubtedly Jenny Diver. [12] Jenny, dressed as a baroness with her lover disguised as her footman, would knock on the door of a great house and faint into the arms of whoever opened it. The entire household would soon be rushing around fetching smelling salts and cups of tea, while her "footman" ransacked the joint. Jenny would miraculously recover, haughtily present her calling card to the mistress of the

---

11   Nasal tobacco, or snuff, was the drug of choice among London's elite. Queen Charlotte, the wife of George III, was an absolute snuff-hound who could snort her way through an entire Virginian tobacco plantation in a single sitting.

12   Jenny was atypical of England's criminal population in that she was a she. Most female crime was committed within the family or, in the case of bigamy, within the families. Between 1782 and 1787, only 12 per cent of those accused of crimes in the Home Counties were female. Women were also less likely to be arrested, and men exploited this during the 1760s London Food Riots by dressing in their wives' clothes before going out to throw cobblestones at soldiers.

house, invite her to tea, and leave with great dignity and several hundred pounds worth of silver plate.

Jenny would scour the theatre district for well-dressed gentlemen and invite them to a room in a nearby inn. When her mark had undressed, an accomplice would burst in and tell Jenny that her husband had returned early. Jenny would usher her new friend into a cupboard and instruct him to hide. The confused punter would emerge several hours later to find his clothes and money stolen and an angry innkeeper demanding that he settle the unpaid room bill.

Jenny also owned a custom-made suit with a false pregnancy bulge and lifelike wooden arms. She would sit demurely in church, fake hands on fake stomach, while she pick-pocketed those around her and stored the loot in her bogus belly.

The world lost one of its great original thinkers when Jenny went to dance for the hangman.

STARCHED-COLLAR CRIME

The British criminal law was built on the ancient legal principle of *Ictus differentes differentibus gentibus*, or "Different strokes for different folks". Prosecutions were brought by private citizens and the wealthy simply paid would-be prosecutors to go away or, if this failed, bought a juror's kid a pony. Local magistrates recognised that convicting a chap with whom one regularly shared an evening sherry was just not cricket. In the unlikely event that a gentleman was convicted, the King could be relied on for a pardon.

Although duelling was a capital offence under the Code, prosecutions were rarely brought because men of quality were forever stabbing and shooting each other in the name of honour. William, fifth Lord Byron, killed his cousin William Chaworth in 1765 over a dispute as to whose estate had the most game.[13] John Wilkes, the parliamentary reformer and baboon owner, was regularly challenged to duels by skirt-wearing gingers on account of his well-publicised hatred of Scotsmen. Pitt the Elder and Lord Shelburne, two of Britain's greatest prime ministers, both fought duels with political opponents, and Lord Castlereagh, when secretary of state for war and the colonies, shot the foreign secretary before a cabinet meeting. Of course, duelling was only tolerated where both parties were gentlemen; the establishment was outraged when, in 1784, a noble was shot by his milkman over an unpaid milk bill.

Occasionally a member of the nobility was such a bastard, however, that his peers had no choice but to find him guilty of something (nobles charged with felonies were literally judged by their Peers in the House of Lords, a

---

13   Byron received a small fine for the offence and mounted the sword used to kill Chaworth on his bedroom wall, earning him the moniker of "the Wicked Lord", a title he revelled in. Byron later escaped punishment for shooting his coachman and hurling his body onto a surprised Lady Byron, whom he believed to be having an affair with the recently deceased servant. Byron went completely mad after his son eloped with his niece, which he believed would lead to deformed and insane little Byrons. He let his estate fall into ruin, chopped down the surrounding forests and murdered 2,000 deer in his parks to prevent his son from inheriting anything of value. After his son inconsiderately predeceased him by twenty-two years, Byron devoted the rest of his life to debauchery and collecting crickets. He left what little of his estate remained to his grandnephew George Gordon Byron, the "mad, bad, and dangerous to know" poet and libertine.

chummy arrangement that lasted until 1948). The Peers politely ignored Earl Ferrers when he horsewhipped his groom and beat his wife in public, but were disturbed when he forced his steward to kneel, shot him in the head and then taunted him for the ten hours it took him to die. Ferrers was stunned by the guilty verdict and outraged that his request for his mistress to stay with him in prison was refused. He was hanged from the neck until dead.

WELL HUNG

There were many colloquial terms for hanging, including to "dangle in the Sheriff's picture frame", "go west",[14] "morris" and "dance the Paddington frisk". Most alluded to dancing, as the short drop used in hangings before 1850 did not break the neck but resulted in death by strangulation, causing the victim to twitch and jiggle amusingly for several minutes.

Everybody loved a good hanging, with tens of thousands gathering to witness executions at London's Tyburn Tree. Mrs Proctor, the elderly woman who owned the property next door, erected private viewing boxes in her garden and could make over £500 from a high-profile hanging. Hangings were a great girls' day out, with women attendees outnumbering men (hangings fulfilled much the same function as today's book clubs).

Hanging was not the Code's worst punishment. Female counterfeiters could be burned at the stake; the last woman

---

14 This term was popularised by village people.

FIG.4: THE HANGING OF THREE IRISH CRIMINALS.

went up in smoke two years after the First Fleet sailed for Botany Bay. Magistrates could order other terminal punishments, such as being hanged alive in chains, injected with the pus of smallpox victims or being bitten by a rabid dog. The worst possible fate was to have one's corpse given to an anatomist, as being dissected precluded bodily resurrection on Judgement Day.

Anatomists were pale, blinking men of medical science who spent their nights wandering around cemeteries with shovels and their days doing unpleasant things in morgues. They would attend hangings in the hope of making off with an additional corpse or two and, if detected in their grim work, would be torn apart by the crowd. Nobody liked an anatomist.

SOFT JUSTICE

With all this hanging, burning and dissecting, one might have assumed that the British had their criminal problem well in hand. Unfortunately, this was not the case.

As most jurors fancied a bit of forbidden pheasant, even a man caught red-handed and black-faced with a shotgun, bag full of dead birds and a sticker on the back of his horse reading "Poachers do it better in the dark" stood a good chance of acquittal. Bleeding-heart magistrates would commonly appraise stolen goods at just below the value attracting the death penalty. The law would not allow the execution of a pregnant woman, so a woman who successfully "pleaded her belly" was usually granted a permanent reprieve to look after her child. And King George III, who was a bit soft in the head, kept pardoning his subjects.

Moreover, the British were increasingly drawn to the ideas of Jeremy Bentham, a liberal reformer who believed capital punishment should be reserved for particularly nasty murderers, with other criminals to be sensitively imprisoned, mutilated or castrated. Bentham, who argued that it was possible to scientifically determine an exact punishment for each crime, was opposed to whipping because the severity of the punishment depended on the strength of the whipper, rather than the sins of the whippee. He spent many happy years trying to invent a whipping machine that would deliver lashes at a standard rate and force.

While everybody thought Bentham's obsessive interest in whipping a bit odd, they were interested in his novel idea that criminals might be punished by imprisonment. Historically, prisons were privately run institutions for debtors and those awaiting trial or punishment. Prison owners skimped on unnecessary fripperies such as sewerage, heating and windows,[15] and chained prisoners to the floor to economise on guards, although prisoners could pay to be unchained and to be given other privileges such as food. Gaolers supplemented their incomes by running prison taverns and charging members of the public to view the inmates. The combination of alcohol, access to prisoners and the desperation of female inmates to plead the belly or obtain money for food meant gaolers doubled as organised sex tour operators.

The Gentlemen's Magazine, in 1767, described English prisoners as "a most wretched class of human beings, almost naked, with only a few filthy rags, almost alive and in motion with vermin, their bodies rotting with bad distemper, and covered with itch, scorbutic and venereal ulcers." In 1777, John Howard's The State of Prisons reported that a windowless cell of six by sixteen feet housed more than two dozen men and women.

---

15 Windows were taxed until 1851 because it was harder to hide windows than money. Tightarses responded by bricking up their windows and Scotland entered a second Dark Age.

Prisons were not nice places, and until the early 1800s they were not designed to meet the long-term accommodation needs of Britain's criminal underbelly. Instead, Britain transported its unhanged poachers and friends of gypsies to America, a punishment based on the peculiarly British assumption that leaving Britain was the worst conceivable penalty short of death.

Americans who did not own plantations – which was most of them – opposed this practice because when the convicts weren't picking cotton or tobacco they were picking American pockets. The British ignored these concerns and happily made their criminals America's problem until the tea really hit the fan in 1775.

THE INCREDIBLE HULKS

Once American independence had removed the transportation option, the easiest solution to address Britain's overflowing prisons was to hang more people. Another was to grant lots of pardons; many women were freed unconditionally and men were pardoned if they agreed to join the army and go kill some Americans.

But magistrates continued to impose sentences of transportation, making it clear that the lack of a place to transport people to was not their problem. William Eden, the under-secretary of state, came up with an ingenious solution to the impasse. In 1775, he proposed that male prisoners be sent aboard "a proper vessel in the river in the usual manner and as if in due course for transportation". This allowed everyone to pretend that the inmates of these floating gaols would be transported on the next high tide and certainly by next Thursday. At the absolute latest. Honestly.

And so the convict hulks were born. Originally intended as a stopgap until the Americans came to their senses and begged to rejoin the empire, the hulks became England's first long-term prisons. They remained in service until 1853.

The hulks were overseen by Duncan Campbell, who was a humane and compassionate man. He was just not very good at looking after his charges. The chained inmates were poorly clothed and fed; no fire or candles were allowed at night, as the ships were made of wood and accommodated some of Britain's most enthusiastic pyromaniacs; bathing was prohibited as unwholesome;[16] and the sick were piled together on cramped beds, with the sickbays positioned upstream so that the waste of the diseased drifted past the rapidly diminishing ranks of the healthy. Twenty-eight per cent of inmates died between August 1776 and March 1778.

The hulks were introduced at a time of unprecedented social unrest. The Industrial Revolution was, quite literally, gathering steam and disaffected Englishmen would riot over anything. They rioted over the price of fish during the Food Riots. They rioted over theatres ending half-price

---

16 The British disliked bathing so much that soap was subject to punitive taxes until 1853. Bathing was still sufficiently novel in 1861 that Dr Harriet Austin published a how-to pamphlet titled *Baths, And How To Take Them*. Some less generous souls would suggest that England is still awash (or, perhaps more accurately, apatdownwithadryflannel) with hydrophobia to this day.

admission after the second act during the Half-Price Riots. They rioted over work conditions during England's first cross-industry wage strikes, when even prostitutes struck against the profiteering of their pimps. [17] In 1780, they rioted over the repeal of laws that prevented Catholics from serving in the armed forces. A 50,000-strong mob demanded the reintroduction of the previous "Don't ask, don't confess" policy and burned down the houses of wealthy Catholics and all of London's gaols, releasing thousands of prisoners.

This social unrest, combined with the return of 160,000 now unemployed soldiers from defeat at the hands of the Americans, led to a spike in the crime rate. Finding a new place to park Britain's convicts was now an even greater priority.

GETTING THE DOPE ON BOTANY BAY

In 1779, a parliamentary committee considered possible new sites to stash the empire's undesirables. Its star witness was Joseph Banks, who recommended Botany Bay for its European climate [18] and fertile soil, a far cry from his earlier description of New South Wales as the most barren country he had ever seen. Banks also suggested that the land need not be purchased from the "naked, treacherous ... extremely cowardly" natives, as they were nomadic and would happily go off and nomad somewhere else.

---

17   They were no longer going to take it lying down.

18   Banks had clearly been smoking some of the more interesting seeds in his collection before giving evidence before the Committee.

The committee didn't like Botany Bay, as it was too far away and lacked mod-cons or indeed, any cons at all. Instead, Britain sent 212 convicts to West Africa, gave them guns and told them to defend Britain's trading posts. This was not a good idea, as the convicts defected to the Dutch and looted the posts they were meant to defend.

In 1783, King George authorised George Moore to resume selling convict labour to America. This was not a good idea, as the convicts mutinied and, in any event, Americans preferred African slaves, who could be exploited for generations, to convicts who could only be exploited for a maximum of fourteen years. Moore lost a fortune.

Later that year, Pitt the Younger was appointed Britain's youngest ever prime minister at the tender age of twenty-four. One of Pitt's first priorities was to resolve the convict problem and he gave the task to his home secretary, Thomas Townshend, a cousin of the tea-taxing Charles. If the Townshends had got Britain into this mess, they could damn well get it out of it.

Townshend, who preferred to be known as Lord Sydney, promptly approved another of the unfortunate George Moore's American ventures. This was not a good idea, as the convicts again mutinied, this time chaining the crew in the hold and rampaging through sleepy Devonshire. Nobody ever tried to send British convicts to America again.

In desperation, Sydney's chief flunky, Evan Nepean, asked Portugal if the British might purchase the Atlantic island of St Matthews to house the convicts. This was not a good idea, as the island did not actually exist. Portugal also declined Nepean's offer to use the convicts as galley slaves, as English slaves went pink in the sun and whinged whenever they were asked to do anything.

Meanwhile, James Matra, an American loyal to the Crown who had served on the *Endeavour*, was promoting the establishment of a colony at Botany Bay. He envisaged it as a safe haven for his fellow loyalist Americans and suggested that Sydney might like to deposit a few convicts there as well, as it was both far away and surrounded by water, which would prevent the convicts from walking back to civilisation.

Lord Sydney was not convinced and instead proposed to send a shipment of convicts 400 miles up the Gambia River. They would be left without any support in a disease-infested swamp surrounded by angry African warriors keen to debate the finer points of Britain's slave trade. Everybody else thought that this was not a good idea and Pitt was forced to accept another parliamentary inquiry into transportation. In 1785, the Beauchamp Inquiry passed over Botany Bay for Das Voltas Bay in West Africa. This was not a good idea, as the subsequent scouting expedition searched the area "without finding a drop of fresh water, or seeing a tree". Much to the embarrassment of the inquiry, it didn't even find a bay.

By now Pitt had had enough and made it clear to Sydney that it was Botany Bay or bust. Two events of 1785 helped inform Pitt's decision. First, the French had sent Lapérouse to sniff around the South Seas and Pitt didn't want to be eating baguette the next time he crossed the equator. Second, Pitt was having problems with his dope dealer.

Catherine the Great of Russia controlled the world's cannabis supply and Pitt needed a regular fix, as the Royal Navy used hemp from the cannabis plant to make rope and canvas. [19] Catherine had ordered Russian merchants to form a cannabis cartel and instructed her spies to buy up Britain's warehoused hemp. She then demanded that the Admiralty buy Russian product at exorbitant prices.

On 18 August 1786, Sydney circulated Evan Nepean's appropriately titled *Heads of a Plan* for the establishment of a colony in New South Wales. The *Heads* emphasised the advantages of the new settlement as a place to cultivate the "New Zealand hemp or flax-plant", which Banks believed to be better gear than the Russian stuff. It also promoted the colony as a potential source of Norfolk Island pine for the navy's ships, and of "Asiatic productions" (cotton and spices).

Australia owes its existence to tea, tax evasion, criminals and cannabis. With these four sturdy pillars as its foundation, what could possibly go wrong?

---

19   The word "canvas" is derived from "cannabis". Cannabis in ship's ropes was phased out in the 1930s with the introduction of Manilla hemp, a fibre made from the banana, finally giving victory to William Dampier's pro-plantain forces over Joseph Banks's ladyfingerphobes in the Banana Wars.

5

A wretched hive of scum and villainy

You will never find a more
wretched hive of scum and villainy.

Obi Wan Kenobi, a long time ago ...

'ELLO GUVNOR

EVAN NEPEAN WAS TASKED WITH FINDING "AN able and discreet officer" to serve as the inaugural governor of New South Wales. He advertised through the usual channels, but Britain's able and discreet officers all needed to stay home to powder their wigs.

So Nepean offered the job to Arthur Phillip, a doggedly unexceptional performer most noted in Royal Navy circles for having two first names. Phillip was the man you would want in your corner if you'd run out of paperclips or your workmates had left unwashed cutlery in the office sink – a man who could boldly requisition new stationery or prepare a dishwasher roster without fear or favour.

Phillip's attention to detail, his fascination with rules and regulations, and his singular lack of humour can all be attributed to his being half German. Having a touch of the Teuton was not unusual in eighteenth-century Britain, where the royal family had been Kaisering it up since Georg Ludwig of Hanover, who couldn't speak a word of English, was crowned King George I in 1714.

But Phillip came from both more humble and more linguistically advanced stock. Born within earshot of the Bow Bells, the governor-to-be was a Cockney. While many of his peers were embarking on a life of crime Phillip swotted under the tutelage of his language-teacher father and could soon say "'ello Guvnor" in five languages – six if you count rhyming slang.

Mrs Phillip's previous liaison with a sailor was enough to get young Arthur into the Royal Hospital School at Greenwich, an institution for the relatives of dead or disabled seamen that took young boys and turned them into slightly older boys who could sail. At school, Phillip was the pale asthmatic kid with flat feet who was always picked last for team games. He caught colds easily, suffered from an assortment of mysterious abdominal pains and was working on his squint. By the age of fifteen he had set his spindly little legs on the road to lifelong hypochondria and, although he yearned for the discipline and well-pressed uniforms of the Royal Navy, was rejected as unfit for service.

Instead, Phillip found himself holding a harpoon off the coast of Greenland. While sperm whales are now only killed for research,[1] in the eighteenth century they were killed for fun and profit. Nightwatchmen needed whale oil to light their lamps, women needed whalebone to hold up their corsets, and Frenchmen needed whale ambergris to make perfume. The governor-to-be spent many happy months spearing anything with a blowhole. Three decades later a whale would conspire in spearing him.

Phillip finally managed to join the navy in 1755, but was discharged on medical grounds the following year. He snuck back in a few months later, as Britain needed as many men as possible to kill the French and it was hoped that the sickly Phillip might take out a few by sneezing on them.

At the age of twenty-four, Phillip married a 41-year-old widow for her money and took up farming and cloth manufacture. He soon separated from his wife, however, and returned to sea, taking command of a press gang. His job was to politely ask poor people if they wanted to join the navy and, if they declined, club them over the head and shackle them in the hold of a warship before they regained consciousness.

In 1774 Phillip briefly joined the Portuguese navy, as the Portuguese wanted officers who could kill the Spanish in English. While bobbing off the coast of Brazil, he was hit in the face with heavy tackle,[2] losing his right eyetooth.

---

1   Japanese scientists continue to study the effect on whales of being shot through the head, cut into thousands of pieces, put in a small plastic box and smeared with wasabi.

2   This remains common in the Royal Navy to this day. In keeping with its English roots, this conduct is known as "teabagging".

This dental misadventure would prove crucial in his later dealings with the Eora of Sydney Cove.

Phillip was forever seeking naval leave to visit French spas, in the hope that sitting in a tepid Gallic puddle would cure him of whichever random ailment he was currently fixated on. His ill health drew him to the attention of Nepean, who also served as Britain's spymaster, and "N" inducted him into Britain's secret service. Phillip was the perfect spy. He spoke fluent French,[3] his health gave him a great excuse for continental travel and, if captured, he could confuse his interrogators by giving them two first names.

Nepean saw in Phillip a mind that was ordered, a tongue that could keep a secret and a hand that could work a plough, weave cloth and beat and shackle the less fortunate – skills that would be invaluable in a fledgling convict colony.

ARE YOU STILL HERE?

Sydney wanted the convicts out of his hulks by Christmas, but Phillip was playing Grinch and deluged him with endless memos requesting additional shoes, scythes and sauerkraut (and that was just the S's).

Phillip also wanted more women. It was originally planned that about seventy female convicts and a few wives of marines would sail south, with the remaining 1,400-odd human cargo to be men. The *Heads of a Plan* recognised that this gender imbalance might cause "gross irregularities and

---

3   Speaking fluent French is easy, as L'Académie française's vetting of additions to the French vocabulary means it has only a quarter of the words of English. This explains why the French are such good mimes.

disorders" (i.e. a bit of gayness), which Phillip proposed to address by delivering any colonist convicted of sodomy "to the natives of New Zealand, and let them eat him". Another suggestion was to round up all of Portsmouth's prostitutes and ship them to New South Wales, where they would be married to convicts by lot, but this option was rejected as the French had thought of it first, having settled New Orleans in a similar manner.

Phillip instead decided to economise by making use of the prostitutes he already had, writing of the female prisoners, "It may be best if the most abandoned are permitted to receive the visits of the convicts in the limits allotted them at certain hours." He also thought he might pick up some women at the Friendly Islands (Tonga) or the Even Friendlier Islands (Tahiti). Just to be on the safe side, he collected an extra 100 female prisoners from country gaols and permitted twenty-five wives and mothers of convicts to join the Fleet. These women were Australia's first free settlers.

Phillip was introduced to his charges in January 1787, as they were loaded aboard the ships. He didn't know one end of a convict from the other, but soon worked out that the leg irons went on the bits that were closest to the deck. His officers were apprehensive about their new shipmates. Lieutenant Ralph Clark, the First Fleet's self-appointed misogynist and hypocrite, was aghast at how "the women convicts lolled on the decks in indescribable filth and their all too scanty clothing". Lieutenant George Johnston, anxious about security, installed additional bars to separate the convicts from the sailors and marines, shortened their handcuffs, and equipped their quarters with state-of-the-art murder-holes so that they might be shot in relative safety.

The First Fleet was one of the world's first examples of a Public–Private Partnership, a business model designed to allow government to avoid responsibility, the private sector to maximise profits, and the consumer to wake up in a dark alley with no trousers and a feeling that he really should have said no to that last drink.

The consumers of First Fleet Inc.'s no-frills transportation services found themselves being alternately shafted by Admiral Middleton, the comptroller of the navy, and William Richards Jr, the private contractor responsible for fitting out the Fleet. Middleton argued that convicts should have only two-thirds the rations of the marines, as they would not expend much energy lying chained in the dark. Richards insisted that the weevils in the cheap flour he proposed to feed the convicts were a protein supplement and that the government should pay extra for them. The convicts found an unlikely champion in Phillip, who threatened not to leave port unless they were given better rations and luxuries such as clothes.

Richards demanded an excise exemption for the rum he was taking to Botany Bay for the sailors on his privately contracted ships, giving birth to the Australian duty-free industry. Phillip sought a similar arrangement for his Royal Navy sailors and marines but was denied, as Lord Sydney insisted that New South Wales was to be a dry colony. After the marines threatened mutiny, Sydney agreed that they should be allowed to drink, but only for the first three years of settlement. The convicts were to be "debarred in all cases ... the use of spirituous liquors".

Phillip finally set sail on 13 May 1787, only six months late. His obsessive attention to detail and inexhaustible memoranda meant that the First Fleet was remarkably well equipped. Sure, it lacked a full supply of women's clothing, but that didn't worry him unduly. The only people put out were the convict women, whom he planned to dress in trousers, and the convict drag queens, whom he planned to feed to the Maori.

THE FOUNDING FELONS

Phillip had asked for "healthy young men and breeding women" for his colony, but was given Dorothy Handland, a sprightly 82-year-old perjurer, and Elizabeth Beckford, a septuagenarian cheese thief.[4] The youngest convict was John Hudson, a thirteen-year-old chimneysweep who had been imprisoned since the age of nine.

Most of the First Fleeters were thieves. Edward Perkins stole a chicken, John Price a goose and Henry Vincent a cask of currants. Nicholas English stole hair powder. John Nicholls went one better and stole hair. William Francis was transported for seven years for stealing a book entitled *A Summary Account of the Flourishing State of the Island of*

---

4   Many First Fleet convicts had stolen food to ward off starvation. William Edmunds was transported for stealing a cow, while Thomas Eccles was exiled for filching bacon and two loaves of bread. If Elizabeth Beckford had joined forces with these criminal masterminds, the cheese and bacon burger would have been invented 140 years earlier.

Tobago. William Brice received the same penalty for stealing a mirror. [5]

Of the 759 convicts, twenty-eight had committed no crime other than handkerchief theft, another seventy-eight had stolen goods that included handkerchiefs, and a further 225 stole other cloth goods (handkerchief precursors).

The First Fleet was remarkably multicultural. There were French convicts, American convicts, Jewish convicts and up to sixteen convicts of black African descent, including Thomas Chaddick, a Jamaican who had rebelled against British imperialism by vandalising twelve cucumber plants.

The male convicts came from a variety of professions, while most of the females were domestic servants or "singlewomen of no trade". Terrified that they would be regarded as seamstresses, these women would sometimes invent occupations to convince magistrates of their virtue. One, when asked what work she did, enigmatically replied, "I serve with asparagus."

Historians have spent a disproportionate amount of time trying to calculate how many of the convicts were on the game. Although prostitution was not a transportable offence, prostitutes were frequently found guilty of other crimes (e.g. stealing their drunken clients' handkerchiefs). Historoskankometric analysis suggests that about 20 per cent of the female convicts had turned more tricks than David Copperfield and a sizeable portion of the rest were willing to try a little back-alley sleight of hand when their kids were hungry or they wanted to buy a new dress.

---

5   You don't actually have to break the mirror to get seven years' bad luck.

Phillip, like the colonial administrators who followed him, held female convicts in particular contempt, complaining that many had "diseases of long standing" and "had been discharged from the Venereal Disease Hospitals as incurable". These "unsatisfactory abandoned wretches", in the words of Phillip, became the mothers of a nation.

THE SPY WHO CAME OUT FROM THE COLD

The Fleet's eleven ships soon left the drear of England behind. The convicts, who had been chained to the walls of their cramped holds before departure, were now permitted to stroll about in the sunshine, whistling happy little convict tunes. Things were looking up.

The only downer was the Fleet's chaplain, the Reverend Richard Johnson, a gloomy preacher who would conceal himself in some dim corner and, upon hearing the approaching footfall of an unsuspecting convict, emerge wraith-like from the shadows brandishing self-help pamphlets. Johnson had a pamphlet for every occasion, including *Plain Exhortations to Prisoners*, *Dissuasive from Stealing*, *Caution of Profane Swearers*, *Exhortations to Chastity* and *Religion Made Easy*.[6]

The boundaries between felon and free were already eroding. Lieutenant Johnston, who had so painstakingly installed additional security to prevent the admixture of seamstresses and seamen, now found that it got in the way of his nocturnal assignations with Esther Abrahams,

---

6   See Adam. Adam is a Man. See Eve. Eve is not. Adam likes Eve. Eve likes apples. Now Adam likes apples. Apples are bad. Now Adam and Eve are bad. Where are their clothes?

a comely Jewish single mother who was into black silk lace. [7] The hatches were removed from the female prisoners' quarters "for reasons of health and comfort" and many of the women soon sported new handkerchiefs, the Fleet's principal currency of negotiable affection.

Lieutenant Clark was disgusted. He kissed a small portrait of his "darling wife, Betsey Alicia" every Sunday and wrote her regular letters about the "infamous hussies" he was forced to guard. Among those marines whose families were aboard, discontent was growing. The Navy Board had allocated their wives and children significantly less rations than Phillip had arranged for convict families. They had joined the marines to kill foreigners, not to watch some fat convict kid hoe into another ship's biscuit while their own littluns went hungry.

The marines would bide their time. And then they would make the convict-loving governor pay.

BOTANY BAY BLUES

Phillip arrived at Botany Bay on 18 January 1878. He had lost only 2 per cent of his convicts, which compared favourably to the 14 per cent lost on the average voyage to America. The livestock had not fared so well. Many of the sheep had died of seasickness and the Fleet's kamikaze chickens had taken out the goats when their coop was blown into the goat pen during a storm.

---

7   Esther was so into black silk lace that she stole twenty-four yards of it from a black silk lace shop, earning herself a one-way ticket to New South Wales.

At first Phillip was not concerned by this loss of food. Joseph Banks had promised that Botany Bay was a land of milk and honey, where golden fields of wheat would spring up overnight and fat young wallabies would willingly hop into the nearest frying pan and baste themselves in their own delicious juices. Phillip had only bothered to pack two years' worth of lunch, assuming the colony would soon be self-sufficient.

Phillip rapidly realised that Banks was a lying bastard. The land at Botany Bay alternated between sand and swamp, there was almost no fresh water, the bay was too shallow to safely moor ships, and "every part of the grown[d] is in a manner covered with black and red ants of a most enormous size."

The ground was also covered with Aboriginal people, whom Banks had assured Phillip were few in number and so painfully shy that they would move out to avoid having to make small talk with their new neighbours. The Aborigines showed no such inclination, so Phillip attempted to "open an Intercourse" with them and "conciliate their affections", as King George III had instructed during one of his more lucid moments.[8] This primarily involved "dressing the natives with paper and other whimsical things" and not shooting

---

8   George, by the late 1880s, had started frothing at the mouth, talking to trees, shouting incoherently in German, and turning up to dinner with his underpants on his head. This was perfectly normal behaviour for a British monarch, but George's physicians became concerned when the royal wee turned blue. George's condition has since been attributed to porphyria (a not very nice disease) or wearing too much makeup (Georgian cosmetics contained arsenic, which, when absorbed, can send you bonkers and do strange things to your wee).

them. There was also some cross-cultural wedding tackle display, as described by Lieutenant Philip Gidley King:

> They wanted to know what sex we were, which they explained by pointing where it was distinguishable. As they took us for women, not having our beard grown, I ordered one of the people to undeceive them in this particular ...

Phillip had expected to meet Aborigines, but was unpleasantly surprised when, just six days after his arrival, he encountered more than a hundred Frenchmen under the command of the haughty Jean-François de Galaup, comte de La Pérouse. Rather than hang around displaying his genitals for the amusement of the natives and being patronised by the French, Phillip packed his Fleet and sailed up the coast to the nice harbour he had just discovered.

NEW SODOM

On 26 January 1788, Phillip named the large harbour north of Botany Bay after Lord Sydney, who was also big and wet. Here, at Sydney Cove, he would build a new society.

It would be a society without money, as that would only give the convicts something else to steal. It would be a society without vice, where alcohol and tobacco would be shunned for the pleasure of the plough and the high of the hoe. It would be a society without shops or trade, where the state would provide equal rations for every man, whether felon or free. It would be a society without cities, where communal farms would house and feed a hardy agrarian people. Phillip had invented the socialist state six decades before Karl Marx and Friedrich Engels threw their first Communist Party.

Unimpressed by Phillip's utopian vision, four hundred of the convicts soon scarpered off into the bush. La Pérouse woke up the next morning to a beach full of English criminals shouting "Vive la France!" while trying to thumb a lift home.[9]

Major Robert Ross of the Marine Corps, Phillip's second in command, was not interested in rounding up escaped convicts or, for that matter, in doing anything that required him to get off his generously upholstered Scottish backside. Ross spent every waking hour devising new ways to undermine the governor's authority. He insisted that the marines' sole job was to protect the colony from any French, Russian or Spanish armies that might happen to be passing through the area.

Ross hated the convicts because they received the same rations as he did, even though they did not have to defend Sydney from hypothetical invasion. Displaying both a meanness of spirit and a lack of understanding of the basic principles of refrigeration, Ross wrote in one of his many letters of complaint, "Could I have possibly imagined that I was to be served with no more butter than one of the convicts, I most certainly would not have left England without supplying myself with that article ..."

Ross also hated the convicts for celebrating the unloading of the female prisoners with an orgy and not inviting

---

9   La Pérouse offered a ride to Ann Smith and Peter Paris, a French waiter who had ended up serving seven years rather than *soup du jour*. Ann and Peter never made it home, either drowning or ending up inside a cannibal after La Pérouse's expedition was wrecked off the Solomon Islands. Australia has always been unkind to European hitchhikers.

the marines. Surgeon Bowes wrote, "The men convicts got to them very soon after they landed, and it is beyond my ability to give a just description of the scene and debauchery and riot that ensued during the night." [10]

Lieutenant Clark had by now expended so much ink in his misogynistic diary rants that he was forced to economise by referring to convict women as "D/Bs" rather than Damned Bitches. He wrote of the newly erected women's camp, "I would call it by the name of Sodom, for there is more sin committed in it than any other part of the world."

God destroyed the city of Sodom in a rain of fire. On the night of Sydney's inaugural clusterfuck, God's vengeance passed over the fornicators and instead fell upon the unfortunate Major Ross, smiting down seven of his sheep and his pig with a lightning strike.

JOB'S TOWN

Ross had it easy compared to most of the new colonists. Scurvy and dysentery cut through the camp like Freddy Krueger at a Year 10 formal. By March, Surgeon White's hastily built wooden hospital housed over two hundred

---

10   Historians argue vehemently about what went down on the night of 6 February 1788. Traditional historians say that the convict women were victims of rape. Feminist historians say they were willing participants and should be celebrated as exemplars of empowered female sexuality. Aboriginal historians say that whoever was doing what to whom was doing it on the Aboriginal sacred site of Warrane, which wasn't very culturally sensitive. Revisionist historians say the convicts all had a cup of warm Ovaltine and were in bed by six. Postmodernist historians say that all of these views are equally valid.

FIG. 5: 6 FEBRUARY 1788 – AUSTRALIA'S FIRST BALL-AND-CHAIN PARTY.

patients. Wild rains ripped through the settlers' rude wattle huts and downright abusive tents. Phillip's house, like some pre-industrial IKEA nightmare, had been shipped to New South Wales in little boxes. The do-it-yourself Government House was "neither wind nor waterproof" and the permanently damp governor developed a pain in his kidneys that would stay with him for life.

Sydney's rocky soil was unsuitable for ploughing, which was lucky because, although the colonists had twelve ploughs, there were no beasts to pull them. The convicts were instead issued with hoes and instructed to till the fields by hand. Marsupial rats descended upon the first plantings of wheat and corn and the few surviving crops yielded almost no grain.

All but one of the Fleet's five cows escaped. The one left behind, insane with loneliness, attempted to kill anyone who tried to milk it and was eventually shot in self-defence. Blowflies, bad weather, poor forage and dingoes wiped out sixty-nine of Phillip's seventy sheep.

The colony's hogs were encouraged to roam outside the new town's bounds, where they were introduced to the niceties of Aboriginal firestick farming. The hungry settlers were tormented by the scent of crackling on the breeze and the delighted cries of Aborigines who had never tasted pig before.

When the hogs were kept closer to home, they broke into the colonists' huts and ate their provisions. Phillip issued an order that any hog caught trespassing was to be killed by the person whose property it damaged, making Sydney even more livestock unfriendly.

Food theft escalated. Thomas Hill stole some bread and was punished with a diet of bread and water for a week. When this did not have the desired deterrent effect, Phillip started hanging people. Thomas Barrett, who had stolen butter, pease and pork from the common store, was the first to hang. Just a month earlier, he had crafted the *Charlotte Medal*, the colony's first known work of art. [11]

Alcohol abuse was rife, despite the prohibition on convicts drinking. Getting hammered was integral to eighteenth-century British life, and the new New South Welshmen would do anything for a pint. Sailors and marines traded hard liquor for soft comforts, convicts broke into the wine stores, and there were numerous attempts at home brewing. Fights over alcohol were common, as were floggings for public intoxication.

Life expectancy in the colony was low, as was productivity. The convicts, who were supervised by overseers from among their own ranks, soon realised that they had a monopoly on the means of production (i.e. themselves) and embarked on a series of successful industrial campaigns. [12] They refused to work standard hours, insisting on a system under which they would hoe 88 yards a day. By 1792, they had negotiated this down to 38½ yards.

Reverend Johnson, a later-day Job, found his faith sorely tested. No one would build him a church, but the colonists enthusiastically erected taverns and brothels. [13] With the

---

11   This was the start of Australia's longstanding persecution of artists, a tradition that has forced Rolf Harris to seek sanctuary overseas and Ken Done to eke out a meagre living flogging hideously coloured tea towels.

12   The workers untied will never be defeated.

13   The colony was remarkably secular, despite Anglicanism being its official religion and clergymen from other faiths being barred from entering the colony, except as convicts. Britain's lowest classes, who formed the bulk of the colony's population, often saw the Church as a sheltered workshop for the privileged younger sons of the aristocracy. The disconnect between the Church and the common man was exemplified by churchmen like Bishop Richard Watson of Llandaff, who refused to live in his diocese because his

colony still not a year old, Johnson wrote that the government should send out another Fleet "to take us all back to England, or to some other place more likely to answer than this poor wretched Country, where scarcely anything is to be seen but Rocks, or eaten but Rats".

THE CONCILIATION OF AFFECTION

When the Eora elders looked down from the nearby hills, they saw a settlement of lazy, drunk, violent criminals with poor accommodation, health, nutrition and life expectancy outcomes. Surely these degraded people would quietly fade away or assimilate into Eora society. If not, the Eora would have to consider an Intervention.

There was one among the pale spirits, however, who was familiar – the one with the runny nose, gimpy walk and, most importantly, missing tooth. The Eora marked a boy's transition to manhood by removing an eyetooth, which made Phillip an initiated Eora warrior returned from the dead. Here was a man/zombie they could deal with.

The governor was also keen to deal with the Aborigines. The colony had a slight legitimacy problem and Phillip was desperate to find the savage with the authority to hand over the title deeds to New South Wales in exchange for a couple of mirrors and a blanket. There were a lot more guys with spears hanging around than Banks had advised and if they ever got their shit together, they could make

---

neighbours would be Welsh, and Dr Lancelot Blackburne, a onetime pirate turned prelate who installed a harem in his palace after being appointed Archbishop of York.

the colonists' lives both uncomfortable and short.

Phillip's desire to give the natives "everything that can tend to civilise them" (the aforementioned mirrors and blanket) and "a high opinion of their new guests" was undermined in a number of ways.

La Pérouse had built Australia's first mainland fort before leaving Botany Bay, writing, "The precaution was necessary against the Indians of New Holland, who tho' very weak and few in number, like all savages are extremely mischievous ... for they even threw darts at us immediately after receiving our presents and caresses." La Pérouse saw the darts of the Eora and raised them a musket, sending a number of them to an early meeting with their ancestors. The Eora did not distinguish the invaders at Botany Bay from those at Sydney Cove and were wary of Phillip's gifts, which in their experience were a prelude to getting felt up and shot.

The convicts, whose opportunities for theft were limited in the new colony, had taken to raiding Eora huts. They traded Aboriginal tools and weapons for rum, rations and clothing with visiting sailors, who took the artefacts back to Britain as souvenirs. In contrast, an Aboriginal man who stole two shovels and a pickaxe was shot.

Phillip wanted to resolve these cultural misunderstandings with the Eora ambassador. The fact that the Eora were made up of diverse tribal groups, frequently in conflict with each other, did not deter him. If the Eora were too disorganised to nominate an ambassador, then Phillip would nominate one for them.

The nomination process involved being shown a mirror, clubbed over the head by Lieutenant Johnston and tied up in the bottom of a rowboat. The unwilling emissary, who refused to give his name, was dubbed Manly. Phillip invited Ambassador Manly to lunch and then, having got the diplomatic niceties out of the way, had him cuffed and tethered in the embassy (i.e. Phillip's backyard). Bilateral relations were definitely improving when Manly revealed that his name was Arabanoo, but his dropping dead covered in hideous pustulent sores was a setback. Arabanoo may have had diplomatic immunity, but had no immunity to smallpox.

A sneeze was far more deadly to the First Australians than all of the muskets the British Empire could bring to bear, with about half of the Eora wiped out by the pox in 1789. Phillip blamed the French, who, despite their philosophy and ornate gardens, were notorious carriers of disease.[14] Today, it is fashionable to blame the Makassans, who were even more foreign than the French. However, the fact that smallpox turned up in Sydney the year after British settlement, and that there is no evidence of earlier infection in communities to the north, suggests the British were to blame.

Thanks to the smallpox epidemic, there were many Aboriginal children for concerned Christians to adopt, so

---

14 Smallpox was distinguished from the great pox, which the English knew as syphilis or the French Pox. The English would name anything they found unpleasant or rude after the French, e.g. French letters (condoms), French leave (leaving a party without informing the host), French postcards (pornography), a French bath (a full body wash), French kissing (kissing with tongues), and French toast (really disgusting toast). The French retaliated by calling syphilis *la maladie anglaise* (the English disease), condoms *la capote anglaise* (the English raincoat), and being rude to party hosts *filer à l'anglaise* (the English run), but stopped there because they liked kissing, bathing, pornography and toast.

that they might be raised knowing Jesus and how to scrub white people's floors. Some of the early colonists were not overly concerned whether a prospective adoptee's family was dead. Lieutenant Clark wrote of an Aboriginal couple: "I asked if they would give me the children for my hatt which they seemed to wish most for, but they would not on any account part with there children ..."

Phillip had now shot, abducted and infected the Eora, who were beginning to seriously regret not placing themselves on the Do Not Call Register after being contacted by Cook. This conciliation of affection malarkey was proving deucedly difficult.

NEW ORDER

In Sydney, a new society was taking shape. The convicts forged relationships with each other and with those who shared their exile. Lieutenant Johnston had settled down with Esther Abrahams and would stay with her until his death in 1823. Lieutenant Philip Gidley King, who had established a small colony on Norfolk Island in the first weeks of settlement, took up with his housekeeper. David Collins, the colony's deputy judge-advocate, eventually shacked up with Ann Yeates, a young milliner from the wrong side of the bench. While Collins's wife was writing romance novels back in England, Ann gave him two sons. And a really nice hat.

Things were looking up for convicts like James Ruse, who had now served their time and were free. Or would have been if Phillip had stopped obsessing about sodomy and sauerkraut for long enough to pack a record of their sentences. Phillip hoped that the convicts whose sentences had expired would forgive him this minor administrative oversight and keep on convicting, because they were jolly good at it.

The marines had now split into two factions. Captain Watkin Tench and Lieutenant William Dawes led a group that wished to work for the benefit of the colony and build relationships with the Eora. Dawes took in an Aboriginal girl, Patyegarang, and produced a dictionary of the Eora language, an eclectic work that omitted many common words but contained phrases including *Gittee gittee* (to tickle under the armpit), *Matigarabangun naigaba* (We shall sleep separate) and *Nyimang candle Mr D* (Put out the candle, Mr D), suggesting that Dawes's relationship-building had been successful.

The opposite faction was led by Phillip's unhappy deputy, Major Ross. Ross continued to feel hard done by, despite having secured a second salary by appointing his nine-year-old son 2nd Lieutenant of Marines. He was indignant that his marines were subject to laws set down by Phillip, rather than to military discipline. When seven of his men were hanged for pilfering from the food stores, he snapped.

Ross encouraged the marines to boycott jury duty, which would have destroyed the colony's fledgling legal system (Phillip believed criminals should be judged by a jury of their peers, as long as their peers were not criminals). Ross was pulled reluctantly into line, but then Phillip established a convict police force that took particular pleasure in arresting Ross's soldiers.[15] Ross made it clear that he thought Phillip had lost his mind.

Phillip banished Ross to Norfolk Island, where it was hoped he could do no further harm. Here Ross introduced a bizarre legal system of his own devising. Whenever a sow died, a formal coronial inquiry was held and, unless a natural cause of death could be established, all the convicts were punished. Ross allocated land to teams of convicts and offered prizes to those who gave him the most corn. The convicts quickly discovered a loophole in the scheme and spent most of their time raiding each other's gardens.

Lieutenant Clark travelled with Ross to Norfolk Island and fathered a daughter on one of the depraved harlots he so despised. At least he had the decency to name the girl Betsey after his wife.

Ross's trip to Norfolk Island had dire consequences for both Ross and the colony because Captain John Hunter, who was dropping off Ross on his way to China to pick up enough takeaway to feed Sydney, ran Phillip's largest ship, the *Sirius*, onto Norfolk Island's reef. The convicts sent to salvage the wreck raided its rum and set it alight. Ross lost all his personal effects and the colony lost its supply ship.[16]

---

15   George Barrington was one of the colony's early police officers. Barrington had picked the pockets of London's rich and famous, once lifting a £30,000 snuff box from Count Orlov of Russia. He was so persuasive and likeable that juries acquitted him of most of his crimes, while the London press made him a celebrity, dubbing him "the prince of rogues". After being sentenced to transportation, he attempted to escape from prison dressed in his wife's clothes. He was appointed a constable within months of arriving and within four years was chief constable at Parramatta.

16   Hunter had a proud history of sinking, having been wrecked off Norway at the age of eight and involved in a further shipwreck before totalling the *Sirius*. For some reason, Phillip still gave him the keys to the boat.

Sydney was running out of food. Phillip insisted that officers dining at Government House bring their own bread rolls and David Collins conducted a judicial inquiry into a convict's loss of a cabbage. Phillip ordered that the colony's dwindling supply of seed grain be soaked in tubs of urine to deter theft, but still "some of the convicts could not refrain from stealing and eating it".

Clothing was also in short supply. Convicts laboured naked to preserve their tattered garments and Phillip ordered a shoe embargo, with footwear issued only to "those who particularly distinguished themselves".

Believing they had been left to starve to death in the nude by an uncaring Britain, the colonists erected a signal post and lookout at the entry to the harbour, "thus fondly indulging the delusion, that the very circumstance of looking for a sail would bring one into view." Even this modest enterprise was thwarted by the Eora, who all sported new red headbands within minutes of a signal flag being raised.

CONTIKI TOO-RAL, LI-OORAL, LI-ADDITY

In 1789, King George III celebrated no longer being mad by pardoning all of the women on death row and ordering their transportation to New South Wales, which it was hoped would inoculate the colony from the much-feared epidemic of gayness. The *Lady Juliana* set sail mid-year, with John Nicol, the ship's steward, reporting that most of the women on board were "streetwalkers" and that "when we were fairly out to sea, every man on board took a wife from among the convicts, they nothing loath".

The Floating Brothel, as the *Lady Juliana* came to be known, arrived in Sydney in June 1790 after one of the slowest convict voyages. She had stopped at numerous ports along the way, so that her passengers could resume their former trade and her officers could claim a slice of the action. The Sydney colonists, who had spent three years bemoaning the lack of female companionship, were distraught at the arrival of "a cargo so unnecessary and so unprofitable as 222 females, instead of a cargo of provisions". A store ship turned up two weeks later, but their joy was soon shattered by the arrival of the remaining three ships of the Second Fleet.

William Grenville, who had taken over from Lord Sydney after the *Lady Juliana*'s departure, was determined to slash transportation costs. The slave-traders Camden, Calvert & King offered him a hefty discount on the proviso that he pay them per convict loaded onto the ships in Britain, rather than per convict unloaded in Sydney. This sounded like a good deal to Grenville.

It was not a good deal for the convicts. Camden, Calvert & King had a financial incentive to keep their slaves alive, as American plantation owners had worked out that dead Africans were deficient in the cotton-picking department. However, Grenville's up-front payment meant that a convict's profitability was inversely proportionate to his or her life expectancy. Who were the convicts to stand in the way of market efficiency?

The slavers realised they could economise on guards by keeping the convicts chained in the hold. They then saved on chains by bolting the prisoners together. Now that they could only move an inch, the convicts did not need all that expensive leg-room. Neither did they need warm clothes, as they would not be wandering about in the cold fresh air. Their woollens and other possessions were thrown overboard, and the extra space used to store food. Food? Hang on. Who said the convicts needed food?

The starving convicts ate the poultices applied to their weeping sores. A prisoner bolted to a corpse would conceal his neighbour's death in the hope of claiming his meagre rations, a ruse that proved successful until the cloying scent of putrefaction gave him away.

The slavers celebrated their arrival in Sydney by staging the world's first production of Dante's *Inferno* on water, having successfully transformed more than a quarter of their convicts into ex-convicts. Emaciated corpses were thrown overboard. Filth-smeared human scarecrows, swarming with lice, crawled onto deck before expiring. Others died as they were loaded into rowboats or writhed in agony from scurvy. The ships' captains set up shop, selling the dying convicts' "unwanted" rations to the colonists. Sydney was kept awake by the triumphant howls of dingoes exhuming hastily dug mass graves.

When news of the Second Fleet reached Britain, the government agreed it was unspeakable and so discouraged anyone from speaking about it. Captain Donald Traill of the *Neptune*, the most infamous of the Fleet's deathships, was put on trial for cruelty and murder, but was acquitted after Lord Nelson said he was a jolly fine fellow. The government had every reason to cover up the horrors of the Second Fleet: it had just commissioned Calvert, Camden & King to transport another 1,880 convicts to New South Wales.

YES, MR AMBASSADOR

Phillip hadn't given up on finding a new Aboriginal ambassador, but potential applicants were put off by the work conditions, which primarily involved being tied up in Phillip's backyard and dying an agonising death. Phillip was forced to resort to the tried and true mechanism of banging some poor unsuspecting native on the head, trussing him up in the bottom of a boat, and rowing like buggery while his friends were still looking for their spears.

Phillip, determined not to run out of ambassadors this time, ordered his men to capture a spare. This proved to be a shrewd move as one of the ambassadors, Colby, soon left his diplomatic post.[17] The other ambassador decided to stick around.

Woolawarre Boinda Bubdebunda Wogetrowey Bennelong, or Bennelong to his mates, was a man of great charm, intellect and humour. He was also a first-class pants man or, during those times he set aside the trousers Phillip had given him, a first-class kangaroo-skin-thong-around-the-waist man. Prone to changing moods, swinging rapidly from laughter to rage, Bennelong loved nothing more than a good fight. Watkin Tench wrote of his new friend, "Love and war seemed his favourite pursuits, in both of which he had suffered severely."

When Bennelong was not abducting Cameraigal women and being speared by their relatives, he was trying

---

17   The post had been hammered into the soil of Phillip's backyard. Colby managed to escape after gnawing through the rope that tethered him to it.

to understand what made the invaders tick and, most importantly, what he could get out of them.

Bennelong soon realised that the governor would do almost anything to conciliate his affection and, while Phillip's officers chewed miserably on their own bread rolls at official dinners, he sat beside them loudly demanding another pig. As the colonists fought and fornicated for rags, Bennelong strolled through Sydney wearing his yellow nankeen jacket or his red coat with silver epaulettes. This seriously upset the convicts, who found it difficult to look down on the black man when the black man was munching on the colony's only bacon sandwich and looked like he'd just stepped off the cover of *Esquire*.

The governor was deeply hurt when Bennelong escaped. But Bennelong would not be a stranger. He was forever popping out of the nearest bush and making polite inquiries of startled colonists as to the health of the governor and his housekeeper, one of the many objects of Bennelong's amorous affections.

Phillip's heart lifted when Bennelong sent him a gift of whale blubber. The clans had gathered to celebrate the beaching of a sperm whale on Manly Beach and Phillip was invited over for sashimi. This was exactly the kind of diplomatic breakthrough Phillip had been waiting for. During the festivities, Phillip's eye was drawn to a spear lying on the ground. When Bennelong picked it up and passed it to the wise man Willmering, Phillip genially approached to take a closer look. The governor was soon able to inspect the spear's shaft in considerable detail but was unable to see the interesting barbed tip that was now protruding from his back. Bennelong scarpered as the critically injured Phillip was dragged to a boat under a hail of spears and stones.

Phillip took his spearing with surprising equanimity, understanding that it was payback for the ills his arrival had brought upon the Eora. He sent men out looking for Bennelong in the hope they might be reconciled. Bennelong eventually returned to Sydney after Phillip agreed to build him a house on the point of Sydney Cove that now bears his name.

Phillip stopped feeling the love, however, when the Aboriginal warrior Pemulwuy speared his gamekeeper, John McEntire. McEntire was hated by the Eora for being trigger-happy on the cultural relations front, but was popular in Sydney.[18] In a colony close to starvation, an Irishman with a dead possum or two up his sleeve was everyone's friend.

After Pemulwuy killed McEntire, Phillip ordered Tench and Dawes to fetch him the heads of two random Eora in a couple of bags he had on hand for just such an occasion. A further ten Aborigines were to be captured and lynched in front of their mob. Tench and Dawes spent several days studiously failing to find any Aborigines, although Tench shot and wounded one from a distance to convince Phillip he wasn't a complete shirker.

---

18   McEntire was a particular favourite of Surgeon White, who was a keen naturalist. McEntire would venture into the bush and happily blast away at any bird, lizard or snake foolish enough to stick its head up, with his dead offerings contributing to the publishing success of White's catchily titled *Journal of a Voyage to New South Wales with sixty-five plates of Non Descript Animals, Birds, Lizards, Serpents, curious Cones of Trees and other Natural Productions.*

Phillip eventually calmed down and withdrew his orders for indiscriminate massacre, but he had irretrievably damaged his conciliation credentials. Bennelong remained in his house on the point, but no longer kept a little portrait of the governor on his bedside table. Pemulwuy remained at large, his name whispered around the campfires of his people.

LAST DRINKS

Phillip, laid low by illness, sailed for England on 11 December 1792. He took Bennelong and a spare, Yemmerrawannie, with him and retired to the spa town of Bath, where he married a 43-year-old spinster he'd met in a library. Mrs Phillip made her husband's remaining years an absolute misery.[19]

James Ruse finally convinced Phillip that his sentence had expired and became the colony's first self-sufficient farmer and land-grant recipient, proving that a Cornish burglar could make something of himself in this new society.

Reverend Johnson continued to be spectacularly unsuccessful at spreading the word. When he paid out of his own pocket for a church to be built, one of the colony's more enthusiastic atheists burned it to the ground. Johnson became the colony's most successful cucumber grower and an enthusiastic advocate of Thomas Chaddick's repatriation to Jamaica.

---

19   She accused Phillip of having wild affairs and conspiring against her, neither of which were in Phillip's playbook. Do not try to pick up chicks at the library. It always ends badly.

Ralph Clark returned home to his darling Betsey Alicia, who accepted that what happens on Norfolk Island stays on Norfolk Island. Tears were shed when he died of yellow fever in June 1794. Major Ross, to the relief of all concerned, died the same month.

William Dawes was forced to leave the colony after publicly criticising Phillip over the Pemulwuy affair. He was appointed Governor of Sierra Leone in 1792 and later became a missionary, establishing schools for the children of West Indian slaves.

Watkin Tench became famous for his sensitive girly diary about his days in New South Wales and is the Australian historical figure that mothers would most like their daughters to bring home.[20]

Esther Abrahams still looked hot in black lace and her lover now served in the New South Wales Corps, the unit that had replaced Ross's ineffectual marines. Nobody would accuse George Johnston and his new cronies of being ineffectual. Their ambition to remake New South Wales in their own image was fuelled by a powerful elixir, a draught that men would kill and die for, a base liquid that they would transmute into gold. Its name was ...

---

20 Although their enthusiasm dims somewhat when it is pointed out that their daughters will need a return airfare to Devon, a flashlight and a shovel.

... RUM.

6

Rotten to the corps

*O God, that men should put an enemy in
their mouths to steal away their brains!
that we should, with joy, pleasance, revel, and
applause, transform ourselves into beasts!*

**Othello,
William Shakespeare, 1603**

THE BACCHANAL OF ST DIONYSIUS

THE NAME SYDNEY DERIVES FROM SAINT DENIS of Paris, the patron saint of headaches and hangovers. Denis was also known as Dionysius, a name inherited from the Greek god of wine, drunkenness and wild orgies. Alcoholic excess is built into the very name of Sydney.

Phillip had attempted to restrict access to "spirituous liquors", but consumption had triumphed over moderation by the time last drinks were called on his rule. And the drink being drunk was rum.

Rum was first distilled by African slaves working Jamaica's sugar plantations. It was then adopted by the pirates of the Caribbean, who used it to mix Bumbo, a manly seafaring cocktail of rum, water and sugar, with just a hint of nutmeg. The pirates' endorsement gave rum serious cachet within the boating fraternity and, after Jamaica fell to the Royal Navy in 1655, British sailors demanded a daily rum ration (although they passed on the nutmeg). The Admiralty happily obliged as the sailors had previously demanded French brandy, which the Admiralty disapproved of because (a) it was expensive and (b) it was French.

British sailors liked a drink. And then they liked another one. The Admiralty knew what to do with a drunken sailor, but was struggling to work out what to do with 60,000 of them. In 1740, it responded by diluting the daily rum ration with water, a mysterious liquid that the sailors viewed with great suspicion. The resulting mixture was known as grog.

Grog was no substitute for straight rum and sailors were prepared to take extreme measures to obtain a proper drink. In 1805, Admiral Nelson defeated the combined French and Spanish fleets at Trafalgar, his victory only slightly marred by being shot dead by a Frenchman and having his corpse preserved in a barrel of rum on the voyage back to England. When the barrel was opened to prepare Nelson for his state funeral, it was full of decomposing war hero and empty of rum. The sailors had drilled a hole in the barrel and enjoyed Nelson-flavoured cocktails all the way back to London. [1]

New South Wales was run by sailors, so the colony's love affair with rum was inevitable. The colonists loved rum so

---

[1]   This is why rum is sometimes known as Nelson's Blood and Royal Navy
       sailors referred to drinking their daily rum ration as "tapping the Admiral".

much that they used the term to describe all liquor. Australians nurse an etymological hangover from the colony's rum-obsessed early days, with "grog" still used as a generic Australian term for any alcoholic drink.

But Phillip's policies and the lack of contact with the outside world kept the flow of the universal spirit to a trickle until the *Royal Admiral* docked at Sydney Cove in October 1792.

The *Royal Admiral* was a British East India Company trader-cum-convict-transport captained by Essex Bond, a canny entrepreneur who successfully combined his interests in sailing, selling alcohol and criminal conduct. [2] Phillip had granted Bond a licence to sell porter, a weak and sludgy brown beer, [3] but Bond used the licence to sell the *Royal Admiral*'s contraband cargo of spirits. David Collins recounted:

> ... much intoxication was the consequence. Several of the settlers, breaking out from the restraint to which they had been subject, conducted themselves with the greatest impropriety, beating their wives, destroying their stock, trampling on and injuring their crops in the ground, and destroying each other's property.

This Bacchanal encouraged the business plans of a young lieutenant of the New South Wales Corps – a man

---

2   All characters appearing in this work are historical. Any resemblance to Alan Bond, whether living or dead, is purely coincidental.

3   Any resemblance to XXXX, Swan Lager or to any other beer or hops-based carbonated alcoholic beverage, at any past, present or future time, owned, marketed, drunk, spilled or forgotten by Alan Bond is also purely coincidental.

whose pathological ambition and overweening sense of self-entitlement would transform Australian society over the next two decades. His name was John Macarthur.

BODICE JACK

John Macarthur's father was an underwear salesman, an unusual career choice for a man whose countrymen proudly asserted that "A true Scotsman wears nothing under his kilt."[4] The Macarthur clan therefore left Scotland for England, a land of opportunity where a man could wear a pair of boxer shorts with pride and a lady who ventured out without at least four layers of hosiery, corsetry and associated gussetry was no lady at all.

Young John was ashamed of his family's humble origins. He desperately wanted to be a gentleman, but the only way a player in the smallclothes game could hope to gain admittance to a gentleman's club was through the tradesman's entrance. So Macarthur opted out of the family business and set about scaling the social ladder with the ferocious intensity that he would later apply to destroying five governors of New South Wales. But no matter how fast or

---

4   The terms "to go commando" or "to go regimental", meaning to dress without underpants, derive from the official (un)dress code of Scottish military regiments. During the First World War, Scots officers on the Western Front would check that their troops were not wearing underwear under their kilts, aided by a mirror attached to the end of a golf club. The kilt was retired as a combat uniform in 1940 – Scottish soldiers had discovered during World War I that mustard gas, assisted by the wind-funnel effect of a tartan man-skirt, played havoc with a Scotsman's naked bagpipes. Some WWI Scots soldiers seeking additional gas protection charged into battle wearing ladies' stockings, which accessorised nicely with their skirts.

high he climbed, the underpants of his past climbed with him. His enemies, whom he collected in the same way that Imelda Marcos collected shoes, relentlessly reminded him of his lowly birth, calling him "a stay-maker's apprentice" and "Bodice Jack".

John Macarthur liked himself and expected others to do the same. He had a sensual face with high cheekbones and full lips, framed by artfully casual cascades of raven hair. Smallpox scars gave him a villainous air, but it was the villainy of a Heathcliff or a Darcy – the sort of villainy that impractical young women who spend far too much time reading are convinced masks a deep untapped well of mas-culine sensitivity. [5]

Macarthur's wife, Elizabeth, had married him because of his confidence, despite his poor financial and social standing. [6] She was both attracted and mildly repelled by John's high opinion of himself, writing soon after their wedding that her husband was "too proud and haughty for our humble fortune".

Macarthur believed that a military career provided the best prospects for social advancement. However, getting shot dead on a foreign battlefield would prevent him from attend-ing the right kind of parties, so he simply refused to fight. John spent 1788 AWOL from his Gibraltar regiment, writing

---

5   They are also convinced that the well can only be tapped by an impractical young woman who spends far too much time reading. And it doesn't hurt to play the pianoforte. Or to have a bunch of silly younger sisters who make you seem far more intelligent and interesting than you actually are.

6   The fact that she was four months' pregnant may have also had something to do with it.

outraged letters demanding that he receive full pay until such time as he might choose a posting more to his liking.

Surprisingly, Macarthur eventually chose the newly established New South Wales Corps. New South Wales was not a sexy posting, and officers with money and connections avoided it like the plague. In India, a young lieutenant might immerse himself in gin and polo, occasionally stirring to shoot a few tigers or loot the palace of a maharaja who had failed to grasp the finer points of British imperialism. New South Wales, in contrast, was sadly deficient in the Bombay Sapphire, pony and mallet, big-game hunting and uppity natives with palaces to loot departments.

So few soldiers wanted to join the Corps that its commandant, Major Francis Grose, was forced to recruit deserters from London's Savoy Military Prison.[7] The Corps attracted officers of limited talent and boundless capacity for corruption, providing the perfect environment for the advancement of a man "as keen as a razor and as rapacious as a shark", as one fellow officer admiringly described Macarthur.

The 23-year-old Macarthur, Elizabeth and their infant son boarded the *Neptune*, the soon-to-be infamous Second Fleet death ship. Macarthur wasted no time in alienating his superiors by complaining that his cabin should be relocated so that he would not have to endure the foul smell and even fouler language of the *Neptune*'s convict women. When Captain Gilbert refused this demand for an upgrade, Macarthur did what any gentleman would do: he

---

7   The prison was later converted into London's famous Savoy Hotel. The inmates would have known something was up when the wardens started leaving little chocolates at the end of their bunks.

challenged Gilbert to a duel. Although both men survived unscathed, the conflict led to Gilbert being replaced by the sadistic Donald Traill.

But Traill also found Macarthur's carping about his cabin insufferable and accused him of using its passage to the deck to eavesdrop on private conversations. So Traill nailed the passage shut, forcing the Macarthurs to walk through a corridor crammed with sick convicts to reach the rest of the ship. After this, Macarthur sulked in his room, periodically emerging to criticise the food. This irritated his commanding officer further, who transferred the Macarthurs to another ship in the hope of a little peace and quiet.

Peace and quiet did not sit comfortably with Macarthur, who exploded into the colony with all the tact of a small arms dealer advertising in *Thalidomide Monthly*. When he fronted Phillip to explain why the Corps had breached regulations by importing spirits, his patronising tone so incensed the normally placid governor that Phillip threatened to lock him up. Macarthur replied, "Sir, you may please yourself. You are the first officer that ever threatened me with arrest. And I give you my word of honour if I am put in arrest, I shall require a full and sufficient explanation of the cause before I consent to sit quietly down under such a disgrace."

Phillip, stunned by Macarthur's hauteur, backed down and invited him to dinner. Macarthur refused. He had learned a valuable lesson that he would apply in his dealings with future governors: treat them mean and keep them keen.

INTERLUDE WITH THE BASTARD

On the day that John Macarthur joined the Corps, William Bligh was sitting in a tiny open boat in the middle of the Timor Sea. It was raining and he didn't have a change of clothes, his lips were sun and salt cracked, and he had a gripping pain in the empty place that had once been his stomach. The exhausted mariner would have traded all his worldly goods (i.e. half a coconut and a dead seagull) for an hour of blissful sleep in Macarthur's cabin aboard the *Neptune*. But the trade would need to be made quickly, because he really didn't like the way the other eighteen guys in the boat were looking at his seagull.

How had it come to this?

William Bligh and John Macarthur had much in common. Both grew up in Plymouth. Both had solid middle-class backgrounds (Bligh's father was one of the hated customs officers who interfered with an Englishman's inalienable right to smuggle tea). And both were complete bastards.

Bligh had learned how to be a bastard at sea. He'd entered service as a ship's boy at the age of seven and, fifteen years later, was appointed master of the *Resolution* for Cook's third voyage. Although Bligh successfully steered the boat home after Cook found himself on the wrong end of the rotisserie, his odious personality meant that he was the only officer not promoted upon the *Resolution*'s return.

Bligh was a short man with an overly large head, weak chin, rapidly receding hairline and gorilla-like body. He would have been the perfect casting choice for one of the more disagreeable Oompa-Loompas. Like many short

men, he compensated for his stumptitude by being aggres-
sive and overbearing.[8] He also had a fouler mouth than a
Tourettes sufferer at the business end of a buck's night, with
his swearing legendary even within bawdy naval circles.

But Bligh had connections. He had married the niece of
Duncan Campbell (the hulk guy) and acted as Campbell's
agent in Jamaica. His service under Cook had also brought
him to the attention of Sir Joseph Banks.

Banks was an enthusiastic advocate of slavery and desperately wanted to increase the economic efficiency of the
African layabouts in the British Caribbean. Unfortunately
the negro would not cut cane unless he was fed, which cost
plantation owners money. While money didn't grow on
trees, breadfruit did, so Banks decided to slash slave food
bills by transplanting this high-yielding crop from Tahiti to
the Caribbean.

Banks recommended Bligh for the job, given his famili-
arity with Tahiti and Jamaica and his reputation as an
excellent navigator and strict disciplinarian. Discipline
would be critical, as Bligh's crew would be doing it tough.
Banks had insisted that most of their cabin space be converted for the exclusive use of the breadfruit plant and that:

> No Dogs, Cats, Monkeys, Parrots, Goats or indeed any animals
> whatever must be allowed on board ... every precaution must
> be taken to prevent or destroy the Rats, as often as conveni-
> ent. A boat with green boughs should be laid alongside with a

---

8   Short Man Syndrome was originally known as the Napoleon Complex. This
     is unfair, as Napoleon was 5'6", which was three inches taller than most of his
     compatriots. Napoleon was actually compensating for being French.

gangway of green boughs laid from the hold to her, and a drum kept going below in the vessel for one or more nights; and as poison will constantly be used to destroy them and cockroaches, the crew must not complain if some of them who may die in the ceiling make an unpleasant smell.

The sailors had to contend not only with sleepless nights lying on top of each other in a toxic fog as the heavy reverberation of the night-drum rained showers of dead cockroaches and twitching rats down upon their hammocks, but also with Bligh's regular explosions of rage. Sixteen men deserted before the HMS *Bounty* set sail and the remaining sailors began to refer to their captain as the Bounty Bastard, a nickname that would stick with him for the rest of his life.

Things worsened at sea. Although the refitted *Bounty* was too cramped to accommodate a full crew, Bligh had found room for Michael Byrne, a blind Irish fiddle player. Bligh forced the overworked sailors to dance to Byrne's irritating Irish jigs for three hours each evening in the belief it was "conducive to their health". The crew sought to avoid this humiliation by obtaining sick certificates from Thomas Huggans, the *Bounty*'s alcoholic surgeon. Huggans, who hated Bligh for ordering him to stop drinking, diagnosed every complaint as scurvy. This enraged Bligh, who maintained that he ran the healthiest ship in the navy.

Bligh also alienated John Fryer, the *Bounty*'s experienced master, by promoting the young Fletcher Christian over him. Christian was an impoverished gentleman whose mother had frittered away the family's fortune on miniature portraits and bonnets. He was tall, dark and handsome with a rough edge, as evidenced by the stars tattooed on his left breast and buttocks. Less appealingly, he was "bow legged" and "subject to violent perspirations, and particularly in his hands, so that he soils any thing he handles". [9]

Bligh had taken Christian on two of his previous voyages and treated him as a favoured son, regularly inviting him to private dinners and giving him access to his liquor cabinet. But Bligh's perfectionist streak meant he was disappointed when Christian failed to live up to expectations, which was often. When Bligh was disappointed, he shouted, stamped and swore, and Christian bore the brunt of it.

The crew of the *Bounty* spent twenty-three weeks in Tahiti, waiting for favourable winds and for the breadfruit saplings to take to their pots. Everybody had a great time, except for Huggans, who drank himself to death. But the good times stopped rolling as soon as the *Bounty* set sail for home.

There are various theories as to the causes of the *Bounty* mutiny. Bligh believed his crew rebelled because he insisted that the ship be loaded with breadfruit rather than semi-naked Polynesian women. Madge Darby, author of the racy *Captain Bligh in Wapping*, insists that Christian was driven over the edge by his unrequited love for Bligh. Richard Hough, author of *Captain Bligh and Mister Christian*, argues that Christian's love was requited by Bligh on a regular basis

---

9   This description was published in the wanted notice circulated by Bligh after the *Bounty* mutiny. Officers searching for the mutineers (Bounty hunters) would approach any man fitting Christian's description, shake his hand and then demand that he drop his trousers and display his backside. Searching for Christian remained a surprisingly popular naval pastime over the next two decades.

and that the mutiny was sweet man-love turned sour. The most striking theory is advanced by Karl Lorbach, author of *The Great Bounty Conspiracy: Bligh and His Breadfruit*, who contends that Bligh had a passionate affair with a tall bisexual Tahitian chief named Tina and secretly masterminded the mutiny against himself so that he would not have to tell Banks that all his breadfruit trees had died.

Most historians, however, accept the Nutgate theory.

Bligh woke on the morning of 27 April 1789. The sun was shining, the seagulls were singing and he had a lovely bunch of coconuts. [10] Or so he thought. When Bligh conducted his regular morning nut inspection, he was a nut or two short. Bligh, with all the fury of a squirrel burgled on the last day of autumn, shouted for the crew to bring their nuts on deck to be counted. When this failed to produce the missing nuts, Bligh demanded that Christian disclose where his nuts were hidden. Christian replied, "I do not know, sir, but I hope you don't think me so mean as to be guilty of stealing yours." Bligh exploded, "Yes, you damned hound, I do. You must have stolen them from me or you could have given a better account of them. God damn you, you scoundrels, you are all thieves alike and combine with the men to rob me. I suppose you'll steal my yams next ..."

---

10   The English are fascinated by coconuts because of their limitless potential for double entendre, the staple of English comedy ever since Oscar Wilde decamped from Ireland in 1874. The coconut craze reached its zenith with Fred Heatherton's 1944 harmlessly risqué classic "I've Got a Lovely Bunch of Coconuts". The Swedes, whose tastes are much darker (see anything by Ingmar Bergman), released their own adaption of the song in 1950. *Far jag kan inte få upp min kokosnöt* ("Dad, I can't crack my coconut open") is the story of a Swedish boy who, in attempting to open an obdurate coconut, disfigures his mother, destroys all her furniture, and finally blows up the family home.

Something in Christian broke that day. That night, he rounded up the most dissatisfied members of the crew, seized the ship's weapons, and led his men against Bligh.

Bligh and eighteen loyalists were lowered into a 23-foot launch and set adrift with meagre supplies of water, rum, wine, biscuit, bread, breadfruit and ... coconut. The launch was too crowded for anyone to lie down and so low in the water that constant bailing was required to keep it afloat. When Bligh pulled in for supplies at the nearby Friendly Islands, the unfriendly islanders attacked his men, stoning John Norton to death. Bligh callously recorded that Norton's death was "a fortunate circumstance, for he was the stoutest man in the ship, which circumstances wd very materially have interfered with the boat's progress and the allowance of provisions".

But the death of the *Bounty*'s resident fatty did not solve Bligh's food problems. Bligh gave Robert Lamb, the young ship's butcher, "a good beating" for eating nine raw seabirds he had captured, rather than sharing them, and had a violent argument with Fryer over the proper recipe for oyster stew. Bligh challenged another of his men to a duel in a separate oyster-related argument. Bligh did not deteriorate as quickly as most of his men, who accused him of deliberately sprinkling bread crumbs into the bottom of the launch when doling out the day's minuscule ration and eating the sodden crumbs when no one was looking.

Forty-one days after the mutiny, Bligh arrived in Dutch Timor, having completed an incredible 6,710-kilometre journey across the Pacific and up the north Queensland coast, the longest open-boat voyage ever completed. Despite this amazing feat, most of the Bligh "loyalists" were no longer on speaking terms with their captain and sailed home in separate boats.

Some of the mutineers settled in Tahiti, where they fought among themselves and shot lots of Tahitians in a particularly vicious civil war. The survivors were eventually taken back to England and court-martialled. Christian and eight of his most hard-core followers kidnapped nine Tahitian women to serve as sex-slaves and eighteen Tahitian men and boys to just do the slave bit. He massacred over sixty Tubai islanders and left a trail of dysentery and venereal disease across the Pacific, giving proof to the adage that you can never trust a man with sweaty palms.

Christian's party finally settled on the remote and uninhabited Pitcairn Island, where sexual imbalance and the poor treatment of the Tahitians rapidly led to the Pitcairners shooting each other, chopping each other up with axes and pushing each other off cliffs. By the time the outside world found Pitcairn in 1808, only one of the mutineers, John Adams, survived. [11]

The *Bounty* story captured the imagination of the British public. Bligh was first hailed as a hero, but as reports of his abusive behaviour emerged, sympathy switched to Christian. [12] Although Christian had been shot dead by a

---

11   A few dozen descendants of the *Bounty* mutineers still inhabit Pitcairn, which remains the world's smallest and most inbred colony.

12   Bligh was believed to have attempted to defraud the Admiralty by submitting bogus receipts for goods purchased in Timor. He also lodged a whopping £283 insurance claim for the loss of his personal possessions after the mutiny, including £59 for port, wine and brandy, and 18 shillings for a dozen nightcaps (of the non-alcoholic variety). The claim was rejected.

disgruntled Tahitian in 1793, he became the Elvis of his era and it was rumoured that he had secretly returned to England. [13] Sightings of the glamorous mutineer were reported for decades.

So what if Bligh wasn't loved? He had his health, he was universally admired as a navigator and he still held the world record for the number of four letter words used in a single sentence. And he'd put all that mutiny business behind him. Hadn't he?

DARK JUNTA RISING

Back in New South Wales, Phillip's departure had left a vacuum and, with no replacement governor on the horizon, the New South Wales Corps rushed to fill it. Major Francis Grose, who assumed the lieutenant-governorship of the colony, immediately demonstrated that he would be a very different ruler from Phillip.

Grose was lazy and corpulent, with stunned-fish eyes and a prodigious double chin that suggested somewhere in heaven a cherub was desperately searching for its missing buttocks. He was outraged that he continued to receive convict rations and encouraged his officers to band together to import additional tasty treats for themselves. Money was in short supply, with Spanish dollars, Irish banknotes and assorted copper coins dribbling into the colony and draining out of it even quicker. However, officers of the

---

13   Christian's mythical return is thought to have inspired Samuel Taylor Coleridge's *The Rime of the Ancient Mariner*. No one ever wrote a famous poem about Bligh.

Corps were issued with bills of exchange to cover their pay, and those bills could be redeemed for sterling in Britain.

The officers bought the cargoes of ships docking in Sydney and on-sold them with mark-ups that would make a used-car dealer blush. Sydney was only just emerging from starvation, and the officers were pleased to discover that the colonists would hand over everything they owned for a bag of rice. Colonists who attempted to deal directly with traders were the victims of unfortunate accidents, like falling down their bedroom stairs in the middle of the night. [14] Traders who tried to bypass the Corps were stopped from unloading their ships and had future cargoes boycotted.

The Corps was determined that the colony's magistrates should not stop its game of Monopoly, so Grose fired them all and stacked the bench with handpicked military officers. The officers used the stacked bench to their advantage, bringing fraudulent prosecutions against those who interfered with their business dealings. The officers accepted payments from convicts to amend their criminal records and provided a boutique revenge service, enabling jilted lovers and other malcontents to buy longer sentences for their enemies.

Macarthur was the calm eye of the Corps storm, untouchable at its centre. He was an early investor in the Corps' racketeering but made his real money by privatising New South Wales. More than any other man, he was responsible for dismantling Phillip's socialist bureaucracy and loosing the running dogs of capital upon the colony.

---

14   Accidents of this kind were regarded as particularly unfortunate because everyone lived in single-storey houses.

FIG. 6: THE MACARTHURS AND THEIR EVIL HENCHMEN
PLANNED TO TAKE OVER NEW SOUTH WALES.

Grose was interested in comfort, not power. Time spent pulling the levers of government was time spent away from the French cheese and racy little Spanish sherry that Macarthur had just imported for him. Declaring "I am unequal to manage by myself", he appointed Macarthur as

Inspector of Public Works for the thriving new settlement of Parramatta.

Macarthur believed that public works didn't. Phillip's government farms only produced food, but in private hands they could grow rich crops of money. The British government had recently agreed that officers could be granted land without resigning their commissions, an unusual arrangement considered necessary to attract soldiers to serve at the arse end of the world. Macarthur, who was responsible for allocating land on the fertile Cumberland Plain, granted the most barren and rocky parcels to freed convicts and the few recently arrived free settlers, reserving the most attractive holdings for his cronies. He took 100 acres of the best land at Parramatta, named it Elizabeth Farm after his wife, and rapidly expanded his property portfolio by recommending further grants to himself. [15]

While Grose advised Britain that these new soldier-farmers were clearing their fields at their own expense, he had in fact granted each of them ten convict labourers, all fed and clothed by the British taxpayer. Subsequent orders from London that officers be granted no more than two convicts each were studiously ignored.

Macarthur was responsible for allocating convict

---

15   Elizabeth Farm is Australia's oldest surviving homestead. Here Elizabeth lived in isolation, complaining of "having no female friend to unbend my mind to". The only woman from her social stratum was Mrs Reverend Johnson, a tedious God-botherer from whom she derived "neither pleasure nor profit". Elizabeth, who had lived a life of comfort as the daughter of a respectable landowner, found herself stranded on the other side of the globe with a bunch of prostitutes who couldn't play the piano, stitch needlepoint portraits of charming woodland animals, or engage in polite drawing-room conversation about nothing.

workers in his fiefdom. He and his allies creamed the top off the labour market, while those who displeased him received farmhands riddled with tuberculosis, equipped with fewer than the usual number of limbs, or unnaturally interested in the colony's limited supply of livestock. [16]

Meanwhile, Macarthur deliberately ran down the public farms. Public convicts received smaller rations and were forced to labour for private landowners in their spare time to survive. When the public housing for convicts blew down in a storm, it was not rebuilt. Most audaciously, Macarthur ordered that the government store was not to accept free grain from the public farms until it had purchased all of the officers' crops.

The officers had been granted free land, their labour costs were met by the British taxpayer and then, in a breathtaking display of double-dipping, the taxpayer was slugged again to purchase their produce. Australian farmers have sought to socialise costs and privatise benefits ever since.

FOOKIN EEJITS

Although they had their pick of the convicts, Macarthur and his henchmen couldn't find enough experienced

---

[16] A steady trickle of animal husbandry cases came before the courts in the early days of settlement. Successful prosecutions were difficult because of the requirement that two witnesses give evidence against the accused – offenders not only had to be deviants, but exhibitionists to boot. James Reece was executed in 1799 for making bacon, as was the unfortunate sow he'd befriended. The colonial courts would also order the death of any four-legged party to such proceedings in accordance with Leviticus 20:15 ("And if a man lie with a beast, he shall surely be put to death: and ye shall slay the beast").

farmhands to tend their ever-expanding estates. Most of the English convicts were city-dwellers whose only experience with a hoe was with a lady who pretended to be really good at sewing. What the farmers really needed were some poor oppressed country-folk. Cue the Irish.

The Irish had been practising being oppressed by English landowners for centuries. Most of them were Papists, which was English bigot-speak for Catholics. The English had themselves been Catholics until 1534, but decided that the Roman Church had lost its moral legitimacy when it refused King Henry VIII permission to trade in his ugly old Spanish wife for his smoking-hot mistress.

The English took their anti-Catholicism seriously. Catholics kept sneaking back onto the throne, so they passed laws that the monarch could not "professe the Popish religion" or "marry a Papist".[17] In Ireland, Catholics were barred from holding public office and fined for not attending Anglican services. Irish Catholics could not own firearms or horses worth more than £5 and were forbidden from taking custody of orphans, to protect vulnerable youth from the taint of Papism. When a Protestant landowner died, his land passed to his eldest son: when a Catholic died, the *Popery Act* required his land to be split among his sons, breaking up the great Catholic estates. The law also required that Catholic churches be made from wood, so that they could be burned down more easily when the local Catholics misbehaved.

---

17   This did not stop King George IV, a trenchant critic of Catholic emancipation, from secretly marrying his long-term Catholic mistress, Maria Fitzherbert. The provisions of the 1701 *Act of Settlement* that prevent the British monarch from marrying a Catholic were still in effect in 2013.

Ireland, in the late eighteenth century, was still a feudal society. Most of the large landowners were Protestant and most of the serfs were Catholic. The English loved to make jokes about the Irish peasantry being a bit dim, and there was some truth in this stereotype. Catholic priests had been banned from educating little tykes, and malnutrition resulted in high levels of mental retardation. [18]

The Irish were not initially transported to New South Wales. Instead, they were sent to Canada, which was the bit of America the Americans didn't want. Irish convicts had an even worse time of it than their English counterparts. In 1788, the *Providence* carried 126 of them to Canada. The eighty who survived the four-week voyage were thrown into the rocky surf at gunpoint; one perished when dashed against the rocks, six died of exposure, and the rest were taken to the Nova Scotian village of Sydney. [19]

Sir Henry Browne Hayes, the sheriff of Cork, sent the first Irish convicts to Sydney (not the Canadian one) aboard the *Queen* in 1791. Most of these convicts had committed the standard crimes – stealing handkerchiefs, wandering about with blackened faces, interfering with fishponds – but some had committed offences that were uniquely Irish.

---

18   By 1780, 90 per cent of the Irish were dependent on potatoes for sustenance. The 1815 *Statistical Survey of Ireland* found that Kilkenny "labourers live entirely on potatoes and sour milk". The poor of County Clare didn't even get sour milk for three months of the year, making do with "potatoes and salt". This diet meant that the Irish poor suffered from "scurvy and scrophulous disorders", spoke slowly and had difficulty tying their own shoelaces.

19   The British loved naming their miserable lice-infested convict settlements after Lord Sydney. Lord Sydney would have preferred sponsoring a town with a cathedral, or at least a nice fountain.

For example, the innumerate or unipedal Mary McLoghlin was transported for "felony of sock".

Some Irish convicts were never tried or sentenced, but transported simply for the crime of Irishness. Irish women, unlike their English sisters, could be transported for the crime of homelessness. Irish gentlemen of limited means, meanwhile, all too frequently "carried away maydens that be inheritors". Abducting heiresses was a peculiarly Irish offence that involved bursting into a ballroom wearing a mask, throwing the nearest heiress onto a horse valued at less than £5, galloping off to meet an unscrupulous priest who would perform a marriage for half a pint of Guinness, deflowering said heiress in a barn, taking her back to her home and demanding that her guardian hand over her inheritance. The guardian would generally comply, as the Catholic Church judged divorce to be a far greater sin than raping a young woman in a barn.

Abducting heiresses was so popular that groups of likeminded Irish youths formed Abduction Clubs. Club members paid household servants to report on the fortunes and movements of potential wives and drew lots to determine which lucky bachelor would get the girl. The club would then help the winner to kidnap his prize.

Sir Henry Browne Hayes, having dispatched the first Irish convicts to Australia, joined them after abducting Mary Pike, who had been left £20,000 by her doting grandfather. He had made the mistake of abducting a Quaker – Quakers took a far more pragmatic approach to divorce than Catholics and generally frowned upon the whole barn business. Hayes was transported for life, but his status allowed him to purchase a comfortable cabin aboard the *Atlas*, while sixty-four of his countrymen died below. Peers of the realm were not expected to do convicty things, so Hayes was permitted to build himself the luxurious Vaucluse House, which he surrounded with 500 tons of imported Irish turf in the belief that grass from the land trodden by St Patrick would ward off the colony's snakes. [20]

The English colonists were greatly amused by the super-stitious Paddies [21] who now walked among them wearing funny hats, smoking little clay pipes and saying incompre-hensible things like "Begorrah". The convicts who arrived on the *Queen* in 1792 reinforced the view that the Irish had spent too long paddling in the shallow end of the gene pool.

The Irish were enthusiastic, if not terribly successful, escape artists. In 1792, twenty-one of the *Queen* convicts escaped Sydney, equipped with a paper compass one of them had drawn, and started walking to China, which they believed lay about 150 miles to the north. Whenever the escapees ran into an obstacle, the one holding the paper would simply rotate it so that the arrow pointed away from the cliff face, ocean or band of angry Aborigines that blocked his path. Then he and his fellow escapees would dutifully follow the arrow until something else got in their way. Watkin Tench

---

20   Hayes was also noted for playing host to the colony's largest moustache in an era when facial hair was unfashionable, having sworn an oath not to cut the hair on his upper lip until he was free to return to Ireland. Moustache growing was a uniquely Irish form of political protest.

21   *The Book of Leinster*, a twelfth-century manuscript of Gaelic literature and mythology, perfectly sums up the credulity of the Irish. The scribe who copied it warned his Irish readers: "Do not credit the details of the story, or fantasy. Some things in it are devilish lies. And some poetical figments. Some seem possible. And others not. Some are for the enjoyment of idiots."

described how these "Chinese Travellers" were later discovered naked, starving and eating poisonous berries. One had died of fatigue, another of spear, and four had been seriously roughed up by the Eora. They had managed to escape an impressive twenty-six miles.

In 1798, another group of Irish prisoners decided to run away to a secret white empire that they believed lay about 300 miles south-west of Sydney, "in which they were assured of finding all the comforts of life, without the necessity of labouring for them". The governor got wind of their plan and, given the various ingenious ways in which previous Irish escapees had managed to die, was concerned for their welfare. And so began the only state-sponsored prison breakout in Australian history. The governor provided the escapees with provisions and an armed escort and told them to be careful. He also appointed John Wilson to guide them to the purported location of the lost civilisation so they could see that there was nothing there.

Wilson was a First Fleet cloth thief who later renounced all cloth goods, preferring instead to wander about in a kangaroo-skin loincloth. He moved in with an Aboriginal tribe, was marked with the ritual scars of initiation, attempted to abduct young Aboriginal and European girls, and took up the name Bun-bo-e. Bun-bo-e had explored all the countryside within 100 miles of the colony and crossed the Blue Mountains more than fifteen years before Blaxland, Wentworth and Lawson. [22]

---

22   Blaxland, Wentworth and Lawson continue to be credited as the first
     Europeans to cross the Blue Mountains because they fit the noble

The escapees soon got tired and asked to go home. The expedition's lasting legacy was the discovery of the koala, an animal whose mindless imbecility rivalled that of the Irish. [23]

David Collins, in recounting the heroic failures of numerous Irish escapees, wrote:

> Could it be imagined that at this day there was existing in a polished civilised kingdom a race of beings (for they do not deserve the appellation of men) so extremely ignorant, and so little humanised as these were, compared with whom the naked savages of the mountain were an enlightened people?

Although the English colonists liked to look down on their cousins from across the western sea, the Irish were initially welcomed to New South Wales. They liked a drink and a fight and were kind of fun. They also knew how to work on a farm without getting paid.

The Irish were vital to the New South Wales economy, particularly as the transportation of English convicts was declining. Back in Europe, a young officer named Napoleon had radically departed from French military tradition. He ignored the time-honoured tactics of *le surrender* and *le run away* and was actually winning battles. England was once

---

explorer stereotype: they were wealthy, had nice haircuts and wore cravats. Australians do not like to think their continent was unlocked by a wild-eyed, dreadlocked, marsupial-clad paedophile.

23   The koala was originally known as the cullawine. It was then called sloth, monkey and monkey-bear before its current name stuck. None of this worried the koala, which was too whacked on gum leaves to care what people called it.

again at war with France and needed all of its undesirables to stand in front of Napoleon's cannons. The Irish were not trusted for this important job because they kept asking the French to help them drive the British out of Ireland. So Irish transportation increased as English transportation slowed.

More than 165,000 convicts arrived in Australia between 1788 and 1868. About a quarter of them, and half of all convict women, were Irish. Australia's Irish population exploded with the introduction of assisted immigration and the influx of tens of thousands of people who liked to get drunk at parties, but who were ideologically opposed to contraception. The rate of Irish immigration and childbirth in Australia's early days means there is a little bit of eejit in most of us.

THE LIQUID ECONOMY

Adam Smith's 1776 blockbuster, *The Wealth of Nations*, urged against government interference in the economy. Smith argued that the most successful societies allow self-interest to flourish, with the riches accrued by the enterprising and ambitious trickling down into the pockets of the grateful everyman. He also wrote, "The colony of a civilised nation which takes possession either of a waste country, or of one so thinly inhabited that the natives easily give place to the new settlers, advances more rapidly to wealth and greatness than any other human society."[24]

---

24   Smith was strangely silent on what the natives get out of such an
      arrangement. Presumably they get a warm inner glow from knowing they
      have done their bit to make the enterprising and ambitious foreigners who

Smith's "Greed is Good" mantra was music to Macarthur's ears. Smith had not only earmarked him for wealth and greatness, but had made it clear that his being an exploitative bastard was, in fact, a public service.

Liquid assets are more capable of trickling down than illiquid ones, so rum became the currency of choice, with the pound making way for the pint and the shilling swapped for the shot. While navy sailors and Essex Bond had slygrogged spirits into the colony from its earliest days, the rum ball[25] really started rolling in 1793, when Grose purchased the cargo of the *Hope*, an American sealer that reportedly would not sell its food supplies unless Grose also bought its spirits. Grose made all the right kind of protesting noises for the benefit of his political masters in London, who still envisaged New South Wales as a dry colony. He then sold the barrels of rum to the colony's officers, who traded it by the bottle to thirsty convicts and free settlers, with mark-ups of up to 1,200 per cent. By the end of the year, the Corps was importing stills to brew money and ruthlessly cracking down on any settler found forging moonshine. The soldiers who ruled New South Wales had earned their infamous Rum Corps moniker.

The colony's lack of money meant that barter was the norm, with farmers paying their workers in sugar, tobacco and, to the joy of their convict labourers, handkerchiefs. But not even the handkerchief could compete with rum. David Collins, who despite his taste for a bit of convict

---

have built a wheat farm on their traditional hunting grounds more successful.

25   The rum ball was "hard currency".

strange was cementing himself as the colony's moralist, glumly reported that the convicts "preferred receiving liquor for labour, to every other article of provisions or clothing that could be offered them". The convicts gratefully received their wages by the bottle or jug and would Bundy on as soon as they'd bundied off.

Collins was convinced that liquor led to other vices, particularly gambling. He wrote:

> To such excess was this pursuit carried among the convicts, that some had been known, after losing provisions, money, and all their spare clothing, to have staked and lost the very clothes on their wretched backs, standing in the midst of their associates as naked, and as indifferent about it, as the unconscious natives of the country.

Alexandro Malaspina, a Spaniard who visited Sydney in 1793, was amazed by all the nude drunks who wanted to play cards with him. He wrote of the colonists' "continued abuse of liquor" and "frequent, at times baseless duels", but believed the colony's moral laxity was most apparent in its women, who "approach announcing the price at which they sell their favours".

The excess of alcohol had a profound impact on New South Wales. One Christmas Eve, two settlers competed in a drinking competition using raw spirits and one did not wake up to find out whether Santa thought he'd been naughty or nice. Thomas Daveny, a convict judged by Phillip to be "a most useful man" and promoted to overseer of the Toongabbie public farm, met his end in half a gallon of Cape brandy. Rumours circulated that the officers were buying the land of desperate drunks for a bottle of rum a plot.

Yet Smith's trickle-down theory proved accurate in New South Wales. The colony was becoming prosperous in appearance, with stately homes springing up between groves of banksia and grevillea. As agriculture expanded, the threat of famine receded. Women who had been unable to fall pregnant after years of grinding poverty suddenly became fertile, and Australia underwent its first baby boom. [26]

The convicts became part of the private economy, receiving payment for work performed outside regular convicting hours. The officers' social snobbery and general laziness prevented them from retailing, so they wholesaled to their convict mistresses or servants, who opened shops and taverns. Convict agents like Simeon Lord soon owned grander houses than the governor.

In 1794, James Ruse left the land granted to him by Phillip and led twenty-two mostly ex-convict farmers to settle the Hawkesbury. Collins wrote disapprovingly that the Hawkesbury settlers "consumed their time and substance in drinking and rioting; and trusting to the extreme fertility of the soil, which they declared would produce an ample crop at any time without much labour".

---

26 In 1801, the visiting French naturalist, François Péron, noted that "after residing a year or two at Port Jackson, most of the English prostitutes became remarkably fruitful". Rather than attributing this to changes in climate and diet, he believed the fertility of the "disgusting prostitutes" was linked to "the sudden revolution in their moral conduct", paradoxically arguing that a reduction in sexual activity resulted in more babies, as "an excess of sexual intercourse destroys the sensibility of the female organs".

The authorities back in Britain began to get edgy about all the healthy convicts drinking rum in the sun while the home-grown poor continued to scrabble for scraps in the smog and muck. The English clergyman Sydney Smith wrote, "the ancient avocation of picking pockets will certainly not become more discredited from the knowledge that it may eventually lead to the possession of a farm of a thousand acres on the River Hawkesbury."[27]

Although the colony had developed rapidly following Phillip's departure, the Corps' days of rum and roses were drawing to a close. Mother Britain had wearied of military rule in her farthest-flung outpost and was preparing to send a plague of governors to blight the House of Macarthur.

---

27   Smith was a towering intellect and moral philosopher and the greatest satirist
       since Jonathan Swift, yet today he is best known for his rhyming recipe
       for potato salad, popularised in *Common Sense in the Household: A Manual of
       Practical Housewifery*.

7

A dish best served cold

Before you embark on a journey
of revenge, dig two graves.

Confucius, circa 500 B.C.

HUNTER BECOMES THE HUNTED

MAJOR GROSE'S DEPARTURE FOR BRITAIN IN 1794 heralded fourteen years of strife and bloody vengeance within the colony. Macarthur fought successive governors, Bligh fought successive crews, the Aborigines fought the colonists, and the Irish fought each other and everyone else.

Governor John Hunter arrived in 1795 with orders to wrest power back from the junta. Hunter, at fifty-eight years old, was well past his use-by date[1] and had no experience running anything more complicated than a ship,

---

1   Before older readers start writing outraged letters to their local newspaper or anyone else who still listens to them, they should note that the average British life expectancy in 1795 was forty years.

three of which he'd sunk. Phillip had sent him back to London to be court-martialled for trashing the *Sirius* and the new home secretary, the Duke of Portland, thought it would be best to offer him a job on land, where he could do less damage.

Hunter had an excellent sense of humour and loved music, painting and long walks in the woods, during which he indulged his passion for natural history. With this sort of profile, one would have expected him to have been over-whelmed with RSVP hits, but Hunter was a committed bachelor and misogynist.

Portland had instructed Hunter to crack down on the liquor trade and ensure that landowners were assigned no more than two convicts apiece, whom they would feed and clothe at their own expense. Hunter failed to carry out these instructions, as he had fallen under the spell of the charismatic Macarthur, who'd shown him a teetotal-ler convict taking all day to dig up a potato on a rundown public farm. Macarthur convinced the new governor that the colony would starve without happy drunks labouring for poor philanthropist farmers who could barely feed and clothe themselves, let alone provide snacks and trousers to the useless criminals they so generously employed.

Hunter was initially blind to the depredations of the Corps. Instead, he blamed all of New South Wales's ills on its women, whom he insisted were "refractory and disobedient" and "at the bottom of every infamous trans-action in the colony". Women, Hunter insisted, frittered away their days doing unfathomable womeny things while their menfolk toiled to feed them. They also kept having children, who were even more useless than their mothers. Hunter begged Portland not to send him any more of these "irreclaimable wretches" and urged that the colony be converted into the world's largest man-shed, where a chap might spend many happy years without ever being nagged to put the bins out.

Others, however, were preparing to move against Macarthur. The first blow was struck by Reverend Samuel Marsden, Reverend Johnson's new assistant. Marsden, who had been influenced by teetotal Methodists, was sent to minister in Macarthur's demesne of Parramatta, where he preached against the Corps's profiteering and distribution of spirits.

With a ruddy face, piggy snout, melon-shaped head and the strength of an ox on steroids – a legacy of his early years as a blacksmith – Marsden was the sort of preacher who believed in long early-morning runs and cold showers. If you weren't into self-flagellation, he was prepared to do it for you, rapidly earning himself the nickname of the Flogging Parson. He saw sin everywhere, gloomily reporting that "riot and dissipation, licentiousness and immorality ... pervaded every part of the colony".

Marsden, though quick to find fault in others, found it easy to forgive himself. He had accepted a generous land grant and spent most of his time tending his four-legged flock while increasingly neglecting his spiritual one. And although he publicly railed against the evils of liquor, he paid his farmhands in rum.

Macarthur, as Parramatta's magistrate, had rudely dismissed Marsden's demands to lay charges against Simon Burn, a convict who had drunkenly abused Marsden on the Sabbath.[2] Marsden never forgave Macarthur and the rivalry between these two headstrong men grew. Both had invested in the colony's first merinos, imported by Henry Waterhouse from the Cape of Good Hope in 1797,[3] and the preacher was soon challenging Bodice Jack from both paddock and pulpit.

His admiration for Macarthur waning, Governor Hunter now began to listen to Marsden, a brother misogynist, and resolved to return the magistracy to civilian control. Marsden replaced Macarthur on the bench. Macarthur took this badly and devoted his considerable energy to maligning Marsden and the other civilian magistrates. But he reserved his most vicious attacks for his former friend Magistrate Richard Atkins, after Hunter proposed Atkins's appointment as deputy judge-advocate.

Atkins was charming, handsome and the best-bred settler in the colony, the son of a baronet and brother to an admiral and a general. He was also a gin-addled alcoholic with a penchant for getting his kit off when drunk, and had fled to New South Wales to escape his circling creditors. When Atkins accused two soldiers of turnip theft, Macarthur requested information about this heinous crime in a letter addressed to "Mr Richard Atkins". Atkins, insulted that he had not been addressed as "Richard Atkins, Esquire", refused the request and sniffily concluded, "It is

---

2   Marsden had the last laugh when Burn was stabbed to death two weeks later during one of his sermons. The Lord moves in mysterious ways.

3   Waterhouse sold all of his merinos, deciding that his future did not lie in wool. Like some of his descendants, he was presumably more interested in fine cotton.

further, sir, necessary for me to inform you that any letters directed to Mr Richard Atkins will be returned unopened."

Macarthur dragged Governor Hunter into the dispute, who advised him that referring to Atkins as a mere Mister was clearly intended "to mortify him as a gentleman, or to lessen him as a magistrate". Macarthur responded that he could not mortify Atkins as a gentleman as he was not one, but:

> a man so deeply plunged in infamy ... a man so vile ... a public cheater, living in the most boundless dissipation, without any visible means of maintaining it ... I will prove that in his public and official capacity drunkenness and indecency are almost inseparable from him.

He went on to accuse Atkins of issuing false notes, highway robbery and indecent exposure while drunk.

Atkins responded to these extraordinary, although probably accurate, charges with the most wonderfully vituperative letter in Australian history, accusing Macarthur of being:

> a dastardly coward ... the baseness of whose heart even imagination, however warm, can hardly portray ... despicable littleness pervades your every action ... Return to your original nothing; we know what you have been, and what you now are; and believe me an honest and industrious staymaker is a more honourable and more useful member of society than such a man as I hold you to be .... viper, you bite a file; the day of retribution will come, and believe me it is not far off, when you shall be dragged forward by the strong arm of justice to public

view as a monster of society ... the assassin of all that consti-
tutes true honour ... you are a leper in reputation, and that you
ought to be driven from the society of all good men least you
should be infectious.

Being a gentleman, Atkins signed this letter, "Your
humble serv't".

Macarthur's charges against Atkins were heard by Marsden, who, recalling Macarthur's own lack of interest in
prosecuting drunks, dismissed them. Atkins was appointed
deputy judge-advocate and waited for the moment when
he might strike Macarthur down.

Hunter, who had now twigged that Macarthur was a wolf
in merino's clothing, begged Portland to recall the Corps to
England, describing them as "a set of the worst, the most
atrocious characters that ever disgraced human nature".
Three years after his arrival, he finally enforced the limit of
two convicts per landowner, but he never found the courage
to challenge the Corps's trading or grog-running.

While Hunter was dithering, Macarthur moved to isolate
him. Pamphlets were circulated accusing Hunter's steward,
Nicholas Franklyn, of trading in rum; Franklyn committed
suicide. George Johnston, who had been appointed Hunter's
aide-de-camp,[4] was shipped back to Britain on charges of
paying a soldier in spirits. The hapless governor increasingly
withdrew into the bush, temporarily forgetting his troubles
by searching for new animals to sketch. It was during one

---

4   Hunter's lifelong bachelor status and interest in the arts have led some
     historians to speculate that he needed no help being camp.

of these trips that Hunter discovered the platypus, which he promptly killed and posted to Sir Joseph Banks.[5]

Meanwhile Macarthur was writing obsequious letters to Portland, claiming that the governor had ignored his advice that landowners should feed and clothe their convicts and had refused his generous offer to pay for the upkeep of 100 of the lovable rascals.

Macarthur was not just economical with the truth: he bankrupted it. But Macarthur's lies were the sort of lies that Portland wanted to hear. On 16 April 1800, Philip Gidley King returned to the colony to tell his old comrade that Portland had sacked him for being a useless tit and that he, King, was now in charge. Broken, Hunter returned to Britain and was given command of the HMS *Venerable*, which he promptly sank.

Macarthur now had one governor's scalp hanging from his belt and had sworn to avenge himself on Marsden, Atkins and the other pygmies who opposed him. He had lived up to the motto of the kings of his ancestral Scotland, *Nemo me impune lacessit* – None shall provoke me with impunity.

INTERLUDE WITH THE BASTARD II

William Bligh woke on the morning of 27 August 1791. The sun was shining, the seagulls were singing and he had a

---

5   Hunter couldn't take a trick. When the platypus was unpacked in Britain, Hunter's fellow naturalists denounced it as a hoax, concluding that a Chinese taxidermist had sewn bits of a duck and a beaver together in an attempt to make British scientists look silly.

lovely bunch of coconuts ... If he were French, he would have thought himself suffering from déjà vu. [6] [7]

Bligh was again doing the Tahiti to Jamaica breadfruit run. Sir Joseph Banks was not the kind of man to admit failure, so he had ordered a second expedition. Neither was he the kind of man to admit he had chosen a complete tosser as expedition leader, so Bligh was again at the helm of a ship overloaded with both breadfruit and disgruntled sailors.

But this time there was no Christian. Instead Bligh had chosen his nephew, Francis Godolphin Bond, as his second-in-command. Bond's hero-worship of Bligh soon made way for bitter resentment. He wrote to his brother:

> ... our relation has the credit of being a tyrant in his last expedition, where his misfortunes and good fortune have elevated him to a situation he is incapable of supporting with decent modesty. The very high opinion he has of himself makes him hold every one of our profession with contempt ... he has treated me (nay all on board) with insolence and arrogance ....

Bligh's men spent their long days at sea lugging breadfruit trees up from the hold to enjoy the sunlight and carting them back below decks at night. Bligh reserved most of the expedition's fresh water for the plants, while the parched sailors were reduced to licking drops from their leaves.

Bligh finally docked in Jamaica six years, two voyages and one mutiny after he had first set out to deliver breadfruit to

---

6   If he were French, he would have thought himself suffering from déjà vu.

7   Unpleasant feeling, isn't it?

the African slaves. The slaves took one look at the fruit, turned up their noses and refused to eat it. There's just no pleasing some people.

PEMULWUY AND THE AMAZING TECHNICOLOR DREAMINGCOAT

Bennelong had done all the things Australian tourists usually do in England: visited St Paul's Cathedral, attended the theatre, boated on the Thames, and stopped in at a museum where he was shown the preserved heads of indigenous people from all over the world. He also learned how to box, play badminton and drink spirits. But his travel buddy, Yemmerrawannie, had succumbed to England's miserable climate and awful food and now it was time for Bennelong to come home. He hitched a lift with Hunter, returning to country in 1795. [8]

Bennelong's homecoming was a difficult one. He saw himself as a gentleman of consequence and when his sister, Carrangarang, joyfully greeted him as he disembarked from the *Reliance*, he berated her for being naked. He told his people he wanted to teach them to love one another and would no longer tolerate them "cutting each other's throats like savages". Bennelong fought a younger man, Caruey, in an attempt to win back a lover, and insisted on settling the dispute with his fists. Caruey speared him in the back and got the girl.

---

8   Bennelong wrote the first known letter by an Aboriginal on 29 August 1796, telling Phillip, "Not me go to England no more. I am at home", a refrain echoed by generations of Australian backpackers.

Bennelong drifted between two cultures and was at home in neither. The Eora accused him of black magic, and he wore out his welcome with Hunter when he speared a soldier who intervened in a payback dispute. He was beaten with muskets and dragged away, his onetime admirer David Collins branding him "a most insolent and troublesome savage".

Bennelong's sense of dislocation was shared by other Eora who sought the comforts of bread, tea, sugar and spirits on the streets of Sydney. The colonists, who had once looked on the Aborigines with patronising wonder, began to see them through a darker twisted lens. Surgeon John Harris wrote, "The Whole Tribe with their visitors have plagued us ever since nor can we now get rid of them they come and go at pleasure." Elizabeth Macarthur, who judged a people's worth by the standards of the debutante ball, reported that, "The natives are certainly not a very galland set of people, who take pleasure in escorting their ladies."

If Bennelong was the broken heart of his people, then Pemulwuy was their fighting spirit. Pemulwuy, who had earlier disposed of John McEntire, Phillip's gun-happy gamekeeper, was a Dharug man of striking appearance. A warrior and wise man rolled into one, Pemulwuy had a flecked eye and clubbed foot, and reputedly got about in a cloak stained with the pigment of each of the Sydney tribes. Pemulwuy's Amazing Technicolor Dreamingcoat led to him being known as the Rainbow Warrior.

An antipodean Che Guevara who smoked colonists instead of cigars, he waged a decade-long guerrilla war against the invaders, setting fire to their isolated farmsteads, their fields and, less successfully, their sheep.[9] His attacks killed over thirty colonists, a blood debt that would be repaid with interest.

The war on the Cumberland Plain was a war of survival. The colonists had built their farms on the richest hunting grounds and waterways, so the people of the plain were left to choose between starving, begging, retreating into the territories of hostile neighbours or fighting back. Pemulwuy went for Option D.

Pemulwuy's ability to appear from nowhere, set fire to a surprised colonist and vanish into the smoke scared the bejesus out of the settlers. He was viewed with superstitious awe, and it was whispered that firearms could not kill him. Pemulwuy was regularly shot and, despite having more lead in him than an architect's pencil case, would relentlessly pursue his enemies as musket balls filled the air around him.

In 1795, a giant African convict, Black Caesar, smashed in Pemulwuy's skull. The colonists celebrated the Rainbow Warrior's death and were surprised when he came back bigger and badasser than ever, leading a hundred warriors in an attack on Parramatta.

Pemulwuy was shot (again) and captured during the Battle of Parramatta. An incredible eight ounces of lead was removed from his body and, because the soldiers admired his fighting skills, they did not execute him on

---

9   The Aborigines, who had successfully set fire to things for tens of millennia, were confounded by the non-flammable properties of wool.

the spot. Instead, they chained him to a hospital bed so that he could recover sufficiently to be decently hanged. But Pemulwuy rose, Lazarus-like, from his cot, snapped his bonds and decamped at speed through the nearest window.

While many Aboriginal people were drawn to life in Sydney, the cultural traffic was not all one way. The authorities were deeply disturbed by reports of Europeans in Pemulwuy's raiding parties and declared several men outlaw, including John Wilson (Bun-bo-e), for assisting the Aborigines in their attacks.

The ineffectual Hunter never got to grips with the Pemulwuy problem, but Governor King was a beast of different stripe. He offered twenty gallons of rum and two suits of clothing to the man who brought him the Rainbow Warrior, dead or alive, and ordered that the natives be "driven back from settlers' habitations by firing on them". King's banishment of Aboriginal people from the settled areas was designed to turn the town Eora against Pemulwuy so they would inform on him.

The Rainbow Warrior was finally sunk by Henry Hacking on 1 June 1802. [10] Hacking was a hopeless drunk and the promise of a year's free booze provided a powerful motive for murder. He presented Pemulwuy's bullet-riddled body to Governor King, who removed the head, pickled it and sent it to Sir Joseph Banks with a covering letter that read, "Although a terrible pest to the colony, Pemulwuy was a brave and independent character. Understanding

---

10   The other Rainbow Warrior was tautologically sunk by French frogmen in Auckland on 10 July 1985.

that possession of a New Hollander's head is among the desiderata, I have put it in spirits and forwarded it by the *Speedy*." [11]

Banks, being a botanist, was used to people saying it with flowers rather than pickled heads, and was thrilled by the originality of King's gift. He replied that Pemulwuy's head was "very acceptable to our anthropological collectors, and makes a figure in the museum of the late Mr Hunter". [12] Today, Sydney Aboriginal elders demand the return of Pemulwuy's head, which, despite being 17,000 kilometres away from his legs, has gone walkabout. [13]

Pemulwuy's passing concluded the Eora and Dharug peoples' large-scale armed resistance. King lifted the banishment order, allowing Aboriginal people to return to the settled areas. He had made his point – Aboriginal bravery and independence would be rewarded with an extended stay on a dusty museum shelf.

---

11   Banks started his impressive Aboriginal head collection in 1793. He gave the first head he received to the German skull nut, Johann Friedrich Blumenbach, the father of scientific racism.

12   Dr John Hunter (no relation to the governor) was another skull-loving buddy of Banks. He was an eminent surgeon and anatomist and brother to William Hunter who, along with the unfortunately named William Smellie, was the father of modern obstetrics. The Hunter brothers and Smellie are now suspected of having arranged the murder of up to forty pregnant women to provide them with corpses for experimental caesareans, a serial-killing spree that makes Jack the Ripper look like a rank amateur.

13   Prince William has now agreed to search for Pemulwuy's missing head, so it's bound to turn up soon. It is ironic that the Sydney suburb of Pemulwuy hosts the New South Wales Police Force's forensic laboratory, which has one of the largest collection of human heads in the southern hemisphere.

INTERLUDE WITH THE BASTARD III

OK, the whole breadfruit thing had been a bit of a flop, but Bligh was not disheartened. As far as he was concerned, any voyage in which his crew did not set him adrift in the middle of the Pacific or make him walk the plank weighted down with coconuts was a success.

In 1797, the crews of sixteen Royal Navy ships mutinied at Spithead. The sailors had not had a pay rise in 139 years, despite inflation having driven up the price of rum, tattoos, prostitutes and other essentials. The mutiny was of great concern to King George, as he was at war with the new French Republic and the British Fleet was all that stood between him and a date with Madame Guillotine. Lord Howe, Admiral of the Fleet, invited the rebel leaders to dinner with his wife and offered them a royal pardon, a wage increase and improved meat rations. [14] The mutineers accepted the deal.

Meanwhile, Bligh was in command of the HMS *Director* at the Nore, near the mouth of the Thames. Just as the Spithead mutiny was drawing to a close, the crew of the *Director* and twenty-five other ships rose up against their captains. The deal struck with Howe was not enough – they also demanded that the King dissolve Parliament and make peace with France. The Nore fleet blockaded London, crippling British trade, and the mutiny's leaders urged their followers to defect to the French Republic. The

---

14   Lord Howe is otherwise best known for disproving the ridiculous claim of
      poet John Donne that "No man is an island".

revolution petered out when most of the sailors refused to sail for France. Bligh's crew were the last to surrender.

Several dozen Nore mutineers were transported to New South Wales, which they considered a holiday in comparison to serving under Bligh. Alas, their fun in the sun would be cut short when the Bounty Bastard arrived in the colony, wearing his shiny new governor's hat.

THE RETURN OF KING

For the moment, however, the governor's hat still sat atop the balding head [15] of Philip Gidley King.

Unlike Hunter, King was a family man – so much so that he had two of them. The saintly Mrs King cared for one of the governor's bastard sons by his former convict housekeeper, as well as for her own children. A passionate advocate for the rights of little bastards, King converted Sydney's most expensive house into a school for orphan girls, which he paid for by imposing a 5 per cent duty on imported spirits. The Australian welfare system was born and its fragile roots were watered with rum. [16]

King also provided a social safety net for convict women who, before 1805, were left to find their own accommodation. As women had limited employment opportunities, this often meant moving in with a man who wanted someone to keep his kitchen clean and his bedroom dirty. Governor

---

15   By 1800 wigs were "so last century".

16   Australian governments no longer rely on alcohol to fund social services, as alcohol is addictive and contributes to a range of social problems. They now rely on gambling revenue instead.

King gave women another choice – they could seek refuge in the new Female Factory at Parramatta.

Samuel Marsden was initially opposed to the Factory, which he regarded as "a grand source of moral corruption, insubordination and disease". However, he became an enthusiastic supporter when he realised that (a) the Factory had the largest collection of spinning wheels in the colony and (b) he had the largest collection of sheep. Marsden's attacks on the colony's "concubines", as he referred to unmarried women, became less strident when they proved a useful source of cheap labour.

King had no formal orders from Britain when he arrived in Sydney, so he simply made them up and blamed Portland for his anti-Corps reforms. He reduced spirit imports, established a public warehouse that undercut the Corps, gave convicts to landowners who agreed to feed them, encouraged civilian trading, and increased land grants to settlers and former convicts.

Macarthur was so unsettled by this erosion of the Corps's profits that he offered to sell his colonial assets to the governor for £4,000 and return to England. King desperately wanted to rid the colony of the man he referred to as "the Devil's nephew", but displayed uncharacteristic indecisiveness in seeking Portland's permission for the deal.

The home secretary was amazed that a serving officer could amass such a fortune and refused the request. He wrote separately to William Paterson, the commandant of the Corps, directing that soldiers be forbidden from farming. Paterson made sure he lost the order.

The relationship between governor and entrepreneur rapidly deteriorated. Macarthur encouraged his fellow officers to refuse King's dinner invitations, which was about as rude as you could get in 1801. When Paterson refused to snub the governor, Macarthur told King that Paterson was behind the dinner boycott. He showed King letters from Paterson that were critical of the governor – and circulated private correspondence from Mrs Paterson that showed her in an unfavourable light.

Paterson challenged Macarthur to a duel. Macarthur loaded his own pistol, in breach of duelling etiquette, and blew his commanding officer away. He then crowed over Paterson's twitching body, which was considered poor form.

King wanted to try Macarthur for creating dissension between himself and Paterson, but knew he would never secure a conviction before a jury comprising officers under Macarthur's thrall. So, as Paterson hovered between life and death, King sent Macarthur to London for court-martial, writing to the Home Office:

> Many and many instances of his diabolical spirit has shown itself ... he has been the master worker of the puppets he has set in motion ... if Captain Macarthur returns here in any official character it should be that of governor, as one-half of the colony already belongs to him, and it will not be long before he gets the other half.

Macarthur turned exile into a once-in-a-lifetime opportunity. King had sent three copies of the charges against him to London – one with Captain Mackellar, a Corps officer who had accused Macarthur of poor sportsmanship in the duel; one with a Lieutenant Grant; and one with

Macarthur himself. Macarthur, unsurprisingly, claimed he had never received the charges against him. Grant's copy was mysteriously stolen from his strongbox. And Mackellar's copy sank with Mackellar somewhere in the Pacific.

The case against Macarthur had not so much collapsed as evaporated into thin air. He was gently chided for shooting a fellow officer and King was reprimanded for sending such a useful fellow back to England. The stresses of office, exacerbated by Macarthur's circulation of lies against him back in London, were beginning to get to King. Mrs King had to hide the Government House drinks trolley, as her husband had embarked on increasingly frequent port binges, aggravating his gout and leaving him prone to intemperate outbursts. The increasingly paranoid governor replaced his Corps bodyguard with convicts.

Meanwhile, Napoleon had cut off Britain's wool supply. Although Sir Joseph Banks had been paying smugglers to run about the Spanish countryside abducting merinos for the King's flock, domestic supply was still insufficient to meet Britain's insatiable demand. Seeing an opportunity, Macarthur wasted no time in telling everyone that he was the only colonist who used sheep for anything other than immoral purposes. He, John Macarthur, sheep-whisperer extraordinaire, would single-handedly save the British wool industry, if the government would only give him a measly 10,000 acres of the colony's finest grazing land and a few of Banks's prize merinos.

It was a testament to Macarthur's charisma that ex-governor Hunter was a strong advocate of this scheme. Banks, however, was having none of it. Having developed a visceral dislike for the oily officer, he announced that New South Wales was completely unsuitable for sheep farming and warned that exporting sheep was illegal. Macarthur, who by now had friends in high places, obtained an export exemption and defiantly bought eleven of Banks's merinos at auction.

On the morning of 8 June 1805, Governor King was greeted by the sight of a smirking Macarthur parking his new ship, the *Argo*, complete with Golden Fleece figurehead, at the dock below Government House. Macarthur saw himself as the heroic Argonaut, Jason, returning in triumph from exile with the mythic fleece that would cement his rule over his kingdom.

Macarthur handed King a letter from Lord Camden, secretary of the colonies, instructing that Macarthur had immunity from prosecution for his past conduct, had resigned his military commission, was to be granted 5,000 acres of the colony's best land and could choose thirty convicts to shear his sheep.

King knew when he was beat, shook Macarthur's hand and gave him the largest land grant in the colony's history. Macarthur named his new estate Camden, in honour of his benefactor, and planted an olive tree outside Elizabeth Farm as a gesture of peace.[17] The peace would not last long.

King was soon informed that he would be replaced because of "the unfortunate differences which have so long subsisted between you and the military officers of the colony". He collapsed from nervous exhaustion and gout on

---

17 And because he liked olives.

the voyage home and died within months of his return.

Macarthur 2, Governors 0.

INTERLUDE WITH THE BASTARD IV

The Bounty Bastard had distinguished himself during the 1801 Battle of Copenhagen and been promoted to command the HMS *Monarch*. Although Bligh was once more in the Admiralty's good books, his crews continued to loathe him. One of the *Monarch*'s midshipmen wrote that Bligh's "manners and disposition were not pleasant, and his appointment to the *Monarch* gave very general disgust to the officers."

In 1805, Bligh was court-martialled for abusing one of his lieutenants and for "tyrannical and oppressive and unofficerlike behaviour". The charges were found part proven and Bligh was admonished "to be in future more correct in his language."

The verdict didn't worry Bligh because, as far as he was concerned, the officers who had found against him were a pack of ████ing useless ████s.

PADDYMONIUM

The colonists no longer viewed the Irish as genial village idiots who liked a drink. They were now seen as genial village idiots who liked a drink and murdering colonists in their beds. William Paterson's wife, Elizabeth, summed up the colony's fast-growing anti-Irish sentiment, recounting her fear of Irish "private assassins breaking into our houses in the dead of night – in which they were all too successful in their own country".

Britain had been deeply shaken by the American and French Revolutions and the republics that emerged from their ashes. This "all men are created equal" and *"Liberté, égalité, fraternité"* business was against everything the class-conscious British stood for. Terrified that the seeds of republicanism would take root in its green and pleasant land, Britain introduced harsh new treason and sedition laws.

The Scottish Martyrs were the first to be transported to New South Wales for crimes such as calling each other "Citizen". The non-violent Martyrs advocated settling political differences over a nice cup of tea. They even offered to bring the biscuits. The colonial authorities viewed these original political prisoners as harmless eccentrics, allowing them to live in their own huts and exempting them from convict labour. The Irish, however, were an altogether different kettle of potatoes.

The Irish were into violence in a big way – and the more sectarian the better. Ireland was riddled with not very secret secret societies whose members dressed distinctively in order to recognise each other. Unfortunately, this meant they were also recognised by the British authorities and members of other secret societies that had sworn to eliminate them.

In 1793, the Orange Boys, a militant Protestant organisation, split from the Peep-of-the-Day Boys, a secret society dedicated to burning down Catholic farms. The Orange Boys, who wore orange collars when going out to beat up Catholics, grew up in 1796 to become the Orangemen.

The Ribbonmen, a militant Catholic organisation, succeeded the Defenders, a secret society dedicated to burning down Protestant farms. The Ribbonmen wore green ribbons in their buttonholes when going out to beat up anyone wearing an orange collar.

Sectarianism was briefly put aside when members of various Protestant and Catholic secret societies banded together with former members of the Whiteboys,[18] an agrarian secret society whose members wandered about at night in bright white smocks levelling ditches, setting fire to haystacks and hamstringing cows on those Catholic and Protestant farms that had not yet been burned down. This new inclusive Society of United Irishmen, led by the charismatic Wolfe Tone,[19] was a militant republican organisation dedicated to burning down anything owned by Britain.

The United Irishmen wore brown coats and a distinctive cropped hairstyle, which led to them being known as Croppies. When the British authorities started arresting anyone with short hair, the Croppies responded by capturing British loyalists, giving them a haircut and turning them loose, thinking this would sow confusion in loyalist ranks. It just made them really mad. The loyalists retaliated by pitchcapping Croppies: conditioning their short locks

---

18   Ireland had many other boy-themed secret societies, including the Greenboys, Oakboys and Steelboys. Boyzone is not an Irish secret society.

19   It helps your revolutionary cred if you have a really cool name. Ernesto Guevera was known as Che, Saloth Sar changed his name to Pol Pot, and Vissarionovich Dzhugashvili purged anyone who didn't call him Josef Stalin. Wolfe's real name was Theobald.

with hot tar, waiting for the tar to cool and then tearing it off, complete with hair and lumps of smouldering flesh.

The United Irishmen did not like this new hair-care regime and, with the support of 1,000 elegantly coiffured French troops, launched the Irish Rebellion of 1798. The Rebellion was an unmitigated disaster. Although laws limiting firearm ownership had been repealed five years earlier, the rebels preferred to fight the British with pikes. The pike was a long spear that had fallen out of military fashion 150 years earlier, but the Irish were traditionalists. It was also considered traditional, when marching against cannons and muskets armed with only a pointy bit of metal, to die a horrible, albeit quick, death. The British regiments and their Orangemen goon squads butchered anyone wearing a brown coat and quickly put down the rebellion.

New South Wales awoke to an influx of rebels. Most of them wanted to put their pasts behind them, but the colonists wouldn't let them. They were Irish – ipso facto they were bloodthirsty murderers dedicated to bringing republicanism and sectarian violence to New South Wales.

Hunter described the Irish exiles as "extremely insolent, refractory and turbulent". King called them "Satanic", and Marsden opined, "The low Irish convicts are an extraordinary race of beings whose minds are depraved beyond all conception and their whole thoughts employed on mischief." The fact that 80 per cent of the Irish convicts spoke Gaelic and kept climbing into small wooden boxes with the colony's three convict priests, where they'd all jabber away in foreign-speak, fuelled the suspicion that they were plotting something.

The colonists drew no distinction between Protestant and Catholic. They tarred all the Irish with the same brush and then, for good measure, feathered them with the same chicken. This drew Protestant and Catholic closer together at a time when sectarianism was splintering the United Irishmen back in dear old Éire. As historian Patrick O'Farrell put it, the colony's "Irish banded together to defend themselves against the charge that they banded together."

In 1800, one of the convict priests, Father Harold, informed Governor Hunter of a planned Irish uprising. Irish republicans had been manufacturing pikes and planned to attack the church at Parramatta during Sunday service, when all the town's soldiers would be present and unarmed. Harold would not name the rebels, so Marsden decided to torture the information out of the colonist with the most Irish name. Paddy Galvin was illegally given 300 lashes to encourage him to reveal where the pikes were hidden, but said nothing, even when the bones of his back were laid bare. The rebel leader, Michael Quinlan, was eventually found drunk at dawn on the day of the planned attack and the other rebels were rounded up and exiled to Norfolk Island, along with Father Harold.

In 1801, Britain dissolved the Irish Parliament and formally unified Ireland with Great Britain. The new Union Jack, bearing the cross of St Patrick, flew in New South Wales for the first time on 27 May 1801. The sound of pikes being sharpened carried on the Sydney breeze.

In 1802, Irish plotters planned to drive captured English convicts into the guns of the redcoats. Those who refused to die for the uprising would be shot by the Irishmen behind them. This revolution never took off, but back in Ireland, the United Irishmen had regrouped under Robert Emmet.

Emmet was confident that this time his countrymen would defeat the British. Irish weapons scientists had just invented a terrible new device that would change the face of modern warfare forever: the folding pike. The folding pike was a hinged pike that folded in half – the Irish precursor to the flick knife. While this made the pike easier to conceal, the hinge tended to collapse when the pike was inserted into an Englishman. Unsurprisingly, Emmet's 1803 rebellion was a complete fizzer.

The Irish love nothing more than heroic failure. It gives them an excuse to write melancholic poetry and gather in pubs to cry while singing tedious songs into their room temperature beers. Inspired by Emmet's brave ineptitude, the colony's Irish gathered themselves to fail, or die in the attempt. Or both.

On 4 March 1804, Philip Cunningham, a United Irish captain, led 220 predominantly Irish convicts from the Castle Hill work camp in an attack on the nearby government farm. The rebels, who had seized weapons from their overseers, planned to attack Parramatta, execute government officials and settlers, plant a Tree of Liberty at Government House, seize a ship, and bugger off back to Ireland. Things didn't go to plan.

The rebels split up to ransack nearby farmsteads, where they seized more weapons and drank the farmers' rum. Two of the pissed raiding parties wandered about in circles in the dark and never made it to Parramatta. Convicts at the other settlements didn't get the message to join the uprising, but informers alerted Marsden and the Corps. When the rebels discovered Parramatta was defended, they milled about for a while and then marched back into the bush.

The Corps was now led by George Johnston, who had been cleared at court-martial of illegally trading in spirits and returned to the colony and the now matronly arms of Esther Abrahams. King had declared martial law and Johnston had authority to shoot anyone who so much as said "Top of the mornin'" to him. Unfortunately, he only had twenty-nine troops and sixty-seven members of a civilian militia, while Cunningham now had about 300 men.

Johnston did what any good military leader would do when outnumbered by a horde of desperate Irishmen. He persuaded Cunningham and William Johnston, another senior rebel, to parley under a flag of truce. He then held pistols to their heads and ordered his men to fire on the suddenly leaderless Irish.

The Irish, who by now should have been used to the English not playing fair, broke and ran. Quartermaster Laycock slashed Cunningham in the face with his sword and left him for dead. The bodies of the fifteen rebels killed in the Battle of Vinegar Hill [20] were left to rot where they lay. Many of the surrendered or captured survivors were flogged within an inch of their lives and sent to establish the harsh new convict settlement of Newcastle, where they were forced to dig coal for their British masters.

---

20   A local Irish landowner gave the skirmish this name in 1826, naming it after the battle in the 1798 Rebellion in which the Irish republicans got their arses completely kicked.

Cunningham survived his wound but was hanged from the steps of the public store at Windsor the following day. Eight other rebel leaders were also publicly hanged, some in chains, their bodies left to swing at strategically selected places throughout the colony, a grim reminder to would-be rebels that the empire would always strike back.

Irish malcontents made a couple of half-hearted attempts to attack the colonists over the next three years, but their hearts weren't really in it. Castle Hill had quieted the calls for Irish freedom and it would be another fifty years before the Irish would again rise up to be soundly thrashed at the Battle of Eureka Stockade.

THE PEOPLE VS WILLIAM BLIGH

With the Irish put safely back in their box, one would have assumed that the storm clouds of rebellion had passed over the colony. But political forecasters hadn't factored in Cyclone Bligh.

Britain wanted a strongman capable of finally pulling the Corps into line and Sir Joseph Banks recommended Bligh as "firm in discipline, civil in deportment [21] and not subject to whimper and whine when severity of discipline is wanted". With Banks in his corner, Bligh got the gig.

Bligh's wife mutinied and refused to travel to New South Wales, so Bligh took his 22-year-old daughter, Mary Putland, as lady of Government House, and her consumptive husband, Lieutenant John Putland, as his

---

21 Banks had been at his seed tray again.

aide-de-camp. Ellis Bent, a later judge-advocate of the
colony, leeringly described Mary as:

> Very small, nice little figure, rather pretty, but conceited and
> extremely affected and proud. God knows of what! Extremely
> violent and passionate, so much as now and then to fling a
> plate or candlestick at her father's head.

Bligh wanted to restore Phillip's vision of a colony
of smallholders tending their turnip patches and taking
turns to milk the communal goat. Macarthur, with his vast
estates and deep pockets, was the living embodiment of
everything Bligh publicly despised and secretly envied.

Bligh put an end to the large pastoral grants that had
allowed Macarthur and his cronies to thrive. King had
granted 60,000 acres during his rule; Bligh granted only
4,180 acres, 2,000 of which were to himself and his daughter. King had also backdated land grants to Bligh and Mary,
which Bligh repaid by granting 790 acres to Mrs King,
which she rather indiscreetly named *Thanks*.

Bligh mounted a concerted campaign to cripple Macarthur's various business ventures and ordered his prosecution
for the illegal importation of stills. When Macarthur was
refused an item from the government store, he wrote point-
edly: "it would be better if he gave it to me and some of the
other respectable gentlemen of the colony; if he does not,
he will perhaps get another voyage in his launch again."

Macarthur was not alone. John and Gregory Blaxland,
Australia's first truly wealthy immigrants, also wanted to
cast Bligh adrift. The British government had promised

the brothers 8,000 acres and eighty convicts in return for investing £6,000 in New South Wales. Bligh gave them 1,290 acres and twenty-three convicts. Of the first three convicts provided, "one was an old man with one eye and one arm, one was an aged asthmatic incapable of work and one was an idiot".

Bligh was not satisfied with alienating the pastoralists. He alienated the ex-convict traders when he gaoled three of their most prominent members. He alienated workers when he imposed fixed wages, with any person asking for higher pay sent to the stocks or given three months' hard labour. He had already alienated the Corps, calling his military bodyguards "tremendous buggers, wretches and villains" and asking Britain to recall this "dangerous militia".

But Bligh's relationship with Johnston was irreversibly damaged when the Corps humiliated his daughter. Mary had been causing a stir on Sydney's emergent fashion scene, as Mrs Bligh outfitted her with the latest couture from London and Paris. The continent's it girls of Spring/Summer 1807 were all wearing French gauze and Mary wasn't going to be seen in last season's dull linen. Europe's fashionistas also wore petticoats, which Mary deemed impractical for the colony's sweltering climate, instead preferring a pair of brief pantaloons. As Bligh and his daughter entered Sunday service, the harsh Australian sun illuminated Mary from behind, shining through her diaphanous gown and giving the colonial paparazzi their first celebrity rude bits moment. [22]

22 This is now referred to as "doing a Britney" or, if the display is for grotesque

The attending soldiers exploded with laughter, Mary fainted from mortification, and Bligh introduced Johnston and his men to his extensive vocabulary of four-letter words.

But it was Bligh's cavalier approach to property that caused the most concern. Bligh ordered leaseholders to pull down their houses and vacate land adjoining Government House, so that he might improve his view. While Bligh had refused the Blaxlands the convicts they had been promised, he found eighty spare ones to landscape his backyard.

Bligh offered Macarthur compensation to quit land he had leased, but Macarthur refused and paid soldiers in wine to fence the land for him. Before they could begin, a government official arrived and informed Macarthur that he had been ordered to take down any fence rails. Macarthur picked up a hammer and provocatively installed the first rail himself. When the fence was torn down and his fencing materials confiscated, Macarthur loudly denounced this and the earlier confiscation of his stills as government theft. No man's property was safe, he warned, from the hypocritical dictator, an attack that resonated strongly with the colonists. Sydney people love real estate – it's all they talk about at dinner parties – and were aghast at the thought that the government might seize their 1BDR/0BTH hovel with double lock-up convict.

Things came to a head in December 1807, when a convict escaped on one of Macarthur's trading ships. Bligh fined Macarthur, Macarthur refused to pay, and the ship was confiscated. Macarthur then refused to feed and pay

---

self-publicity, "doing a Lindsay".

the ship's crew, declaring that they were the governor's responsibility.

Bligh now had a marauding band of starving sailors on his hands, and they were terrorising Sydney. He ordered a warrant for Macarthur's arrest on charges of unlawfully permitting his sailors to go ashore. Macarthur reminded Bligh that they were now *his* sailors and wrote of the warrant, "I consider it with scorn and contempt, as I do the persons who have directed it be executed."

Macarthur was arrested and brought before the criminal court, which comprised six officers of the Corps and Richard Atkins. The 25 January 1808 trial immediately degenerated into farce. Macarthur claimed that Atkins was prejudiced against him and owed him money and should therefore be removed from hearing the case. When the officers agreed with this argument, Atkins shouted that he would gaol Macarthur. One of the officers retorted that he would gaol Atkins. The soldiers who packed the public gallery cheered and Atkins scurried away to consult the governor. Bligh demanded that George Johnston come and bring his men into line. Johnston refused on the grounds that he had been drunk the night before and had injured himself by rolling his carriage in Australia's first recorded drink-driving accident. Macarthur was gaoled and Bligh threatened to charge the officers who refused to hear the case with inciting treason.

Bligh had just declared open war on the Corps. Johnston popped a Berocca, travelled to the barracks and ordered his soldiers to spring Macarthur from prison. Macarthur, the Blaxlands and over 140 colonists signed a letter calling on Johnston to arrest the governor and assume command of the colony.

On the evening of 26 January 1808, twenty years to the day after the colony was founded, George Johnston, the first European to set foot on Sydney's shores and the man who had put down the rebellion at Vinegar Hill, led 300 soldiers against Bligh in Australia's only military coup. [23]

The Rum Rebellion [24] was a curiously laid back affair, with the soldiers of the Corps singing and playing musical instruments as they marched on Government House. The only armed resistance came in the small and determined form of Bligh's daughter, whose husband had succumbed to tuberculosis just days earlier. Shrieking with grief and fury, Mary assaulted the soldiers with her parasol. [25]

When they entered Government House, Bligh was nowhere to be seen. And so began a two-hour game of hide-and-seek, which ended, according to the rebels, when

---

23   There is now evidence that Bligh carried a "mutiny gene". In 2012, the entire state of Queensland mutinied against Bligh's descendant, Premier Anna Bligh, giving her government the largest electoral defeat in Queensland's history.

24   Bligh attempted to characterise the coup against him as revenge for his efforts to curb the spirit trade, while Johnston and the other rebels maintained it was because he was an insufferable twat. In 1855, William Howitt, a rabid teetotaller who blamed all of the evils of the world on alcohol, drank Bligh's rum-spiked Kool-Aid and renamed the Great Rebellion of 1808 the Rum Rebellion. The name stuck.

25   There is something quintessentially Australian about the 1808 revolution. The Americans have the midnight ride of Paul Revere and the Declaration of Independence. The French have the storming of the Bastille and the execution of a king. The Russians have Lenin, Trotsky and six years of starvation, terror and mass murder. We have a bit of a sing-along and a crazy chick with a small paper umbrella.

Bligh was found quivering under his bed. Bligh must have wished he'd bought a futon, because, despite his protestations that he was just hiding his papers, he was mocked for cowardice for the rest of his life. George Johnston now ruled New South Wales and Esther Abrahams, the one-time Jewish single mother cum lace thief, was the colony's first lady. The colonists celebrated Bligh's fall with an all-night party, burning effigies of the Bastard, tucking into giant platters of freshly roasted sheep, and drinking vast quantities of rum.

Some find it disturbing that these events took place on Australia Day. But celebrating the national holiday with fighting, disrespect for authority, a barbie and a piss-up? You can't get more Australian than that.

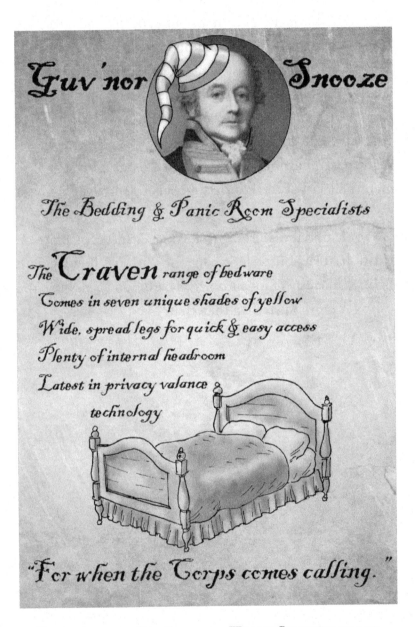

FIG. 7: AFTER THE RUM REBELLION, WILLIAM BLIGH WAS ABLE TO
ESTABLISH A SUCCESSFUL NEW CAREER IN MANCHESTER.

8

I still call Australia New Holland

AUSTRALIA

Matthew Flinders, 1804

GOING DUTCH

PEDANTS WILL POINT OUT THAT THE RUM Rebellion couldn't have taken place on Australia Day because Australia was not yet Australia, but some other place called New Holland. The irritating thing about pedants is that they are almost always right.

The Australian continent had been known as New Holland since the Dutch seafarer Abel Tasman popped over to complain about the lack of facilities in 1644. The Dutch were a direct people who called a spade a *schup* and were not terribly inventive when it came to naming things. If they established a company to trade in the East Indies, they'd call it the Dutch East India Company. If they discovered a big island, they'd call it Groote Eylandt (Big Island).

When the Dutch got adventurous, they'd name their discoveries after bits of the Netherlands and, when they were really on fire, insert the word *Nieuw* (New) first. The Netherlands is small, which meant Dutch explorers gave the same names to lots of different places. They had christened their Brazilian territories New Holland in the 1630s but Tasman, stuck for ideas, happily recycled the name a decade later. Tasman went on to discover New Zealand, which was named after the Dutch province of Zeeland, or the bit of New Guinea the Dutch had previously named New Zealand, or perhaps Zeelandia, which is what the Dutch called their settlement in Taiwan.[1]

Still, the colonists should have been grateful that the continent no longer bore the pre-1644 Dutch name. Tasman had been dispatched to Australian waters to further Dutch knowledge of "all the totally unknown provinces of Beach", a name that reflected the Dutch assessment that the continent was covered in useless sand that no one would buy from them. At least the colonists could fall asleep at night knowing they weren't known as sons of Beach.

The colonists wanted a new name for the land they inhabited, but coming up with something suitably clever and British was lower down their list of priorities than not starving, not being swept away by the deluges that regularly swept through the floodplain on which they had cleverly built their settlements, and not being speared or set alight by the locals.

---

1   According to accepted Dutch nomenclature, Australia and New Zealand should have been named New New Holland and New New New Zealand.

Still, a new name was definitely on the agenda. And it wasn't as if the Dutch could do anything about it. The Netherlands had been on the decline since the great tulip collapse of 1637. The Dutch had lost New Holland (the Brazilian one) to the Portuguese in 1661, Zeelandia to the Chinese in 1662, and New Netherland and its capital, New Amsterdam, to the British in 1674. [2] The French, having successfully conquered themselves in 1789, [3] surprised everyone by overrunning the Netherlands in 1795. The bankrupt Dutch East India Company was wound up five years later.

The Dutch were no longer able to go traipsing around the globe nailing kitchenware to posts, which, quite frankly, everybody else had grown pretty tired of. After they regained their independence from the French in 1813, the Dutch mostly stayed at home, smoking funny cigarettes and producing pornography. [4]

In 1804, with the Dutch safely under Napoleon's jacquesboot, an enterprising young sailor first called Australia Australia so that we can still call it home. His name was Matthew Flinders. [5]

---

2   The British, who were really not much better at naming things than the
    Dutch, incorporated New Netherland into New England and renamed New
    Amsterdam New York.

3   The French had finally found an enemy they were unable to run away from.
    This self-defeating experience was lauded by French existentialists. It was also
    welcomed by French absurdists, who were proud that the Revolution started
    in an indoor tennis court with the swearing of the Tennis Court Oath. The
    French still celebrate the French Revolution as their greatest military victory.

4   The Dutch claim this is art, pointing out that Rubens started producing
    the critically acclaimed *Big and Busty: Home Girls of Holland* series in the late
    sixteenth century.

5   It is not strictly true that Flinders was the first person to name the continent

MATT AND HIS CAT

Australia has more statues of Matthew Flinders than of any other man. It also has more statues of Matthew Flinders's cat, Trim, than of any other cat. Yet most Australians know little of the man who gave them their name, and even less of his fearless feline friend.

Flinders ran away to sea at the age of fifteen after reading *Robinson Crusoe*. He soon signed as a midshipman on the second breadfruit voyage during which Bligh tutored him in navigation and swearing. In Tahiti, Flinders entertained the locals with his flute playing and, if his purchase of a large quantity of mercury from the ship's surgeon is anything to go by, caught a dose of the clap.

Flinders travelled to New South Wales in 1795, shipping out on the same boat as the returning Bennelong and an aspiring young surgeon, George Bass, who would go down in history as the first man to dissect a wombat.

Bass and Flinders soon discovered a shared passion for boating and exploring and became something of a double act. Bass had brought his beloved *Tom Thumb*, a tiny eight-foot boat, to the colony and invited Flinders out sailing. The intrepid duo decided to re-explore Botany Bay and, for their second expedition in *Tom Thumb II*, to re-re-explore it before popping down the south coast for the weekend.

Australia. The name had previously been applied to the general South Pacific area and the naturalists Sir James Smith and George Shaw referred to "the vast island, or rather continent, of Australia, Australasia or New Holland" in their 1793 *Zoology and Botany of New Holland*, although running through a few names before settling on the Dutch one doesn't really count.

Here they encountered a band of hostile Aborigines, but Flinders defused the situation by producing a pair of scissors and offering their would-be assailants free haircuts.

Bass went sailing without Flinders in 1797 and explored the colony's south-eastern coastline. His failure to run into Van Diemen's Land led him to speculate that it might be an island and Governor Hunter gave Flinders (now a lieutenant) a bigger boat so that he could test this theory. Bass came along for the ride and dissected an echidna and some seals while Flinders mapped the coastline, confirming that a body of water separated Van Diemen's Land from the mainland. He named it Bass Strait.

In 1799, Flinders sailed to the Cape of Good Hope. A kitten fell overboard during this voyage but managed to swim back to the ship and scale a rope. Flinders, who had been afraid to get a pet while Bass was around, adopted the courageous kitty and named it Trim after the servant in *Tristram Shandy* (his second-favourite book after *Robinson Crusoe*).

Flinders and Trim travelled to England in 1801, where Flinders married Ann Chappell, a short, older woman whom smallpox had blinded in one eye. The young mariner and his cat sailed back to New Holland three months after the wedding, with Flinders in command of his biggest boat yet, the *Investigator*.

Sir Joseph Banks had sponsored the *Investigator* mission as part of a scientific arms race against the French. Although Britain and France were at war, both believed in science and issued passports to each other's poindexters. In 1796, Banks arranged a British passport for Nicolas Baudin, allowing the French explorer and naturalist to collect specimens in the

Caribbean. The British establishment laughed off Baudin's expedition, mainly because his ship was named the *Fanny*, but Banks was increasingly worried that Napoleon's crack eggheads were out-boffinning Britain's. The *merde* really hit *le ventilateur* when Baudin was sent to survey the as yet unclaimed (except by Aborigines) southern and western coasts of New Holland.

Flinders, equipped with *un passeport français*, sailed after Baudin with orders to chart this coastline too and conclusively settle whether it and New South Wales were part of the same continent. He encountered Baudin at South Australia's conveniently named Encounter Bay on 8 April 1802. While Flinders spoke limited French, and Baudin refused to speak English because that's what French people do, the two seafarers got on well and wished each other luck. Flinders and Trim went on to become the first man and cat to circumnavigate Australia, while Baudin named southern Australia *Terre Napoleon*. Nobody except the French took this seriously and Baudin abandoned his expedition in Sydney after scurvy killed a tenth of his crew and the ship's monkey. [6]

Flinders and Trim set sail for England, but only made it 700 miles before wrecking their ship on the inconveniently named Wreck Reef. After a miserable rowboat trip back to Sydney, Flinders and his plucky pussy again struck out for home, this time aboard the *Cumberland*. The ship had to put in at Mauritius for repairs and Flinders, despite his French passport, was arrested. Charles Decaen, the island's French

---

6   This is one of the earliest historical records of a surrender monkey.

governor, accused Flinders of carrying military documents and claimed that the passport was invalid because it only authorised travel aboard the *Investigator*. These charges were mere pretexts. Decaen had arrested Flinders for the far more serious crime of bad manners – he was furious that Flinders had failed to remove his hat before addressing him and had refused an invitation to dine with Madame Decaen.

The vindictive governor ignored Napoleon's order to release Flinders and kept him imprisoned for seven years, during which time Trim mysteriously disappeared. Flinders offered a princely ten guineas for the return of the missing moggy, but eventually reconciled himself to the fact that his cat had been eaten by the French.

In 1804 Flinders wrote to Banks, enclosing a map of the continent he had recently charted labelled "AUSTRALIA". Banks hated the name because he was a botanist and botanists liked double-barrelled Latin names for things; he wanted to call the continent *Terra Australis*.

Flinders was finally released in 1810 and returned to England a broken man. The French had claimed credit for his maps, he had little money, and he suffered from "the gravelly", an agonising venereal legacy that left him peeing gravel-like crystals. He spent the next four years hiding from his wife in the attic, preparing his charts and manuscripts for publication. Banks had convinced him to call his book *A Voyage to Terra Australis*, although Flinders included a footnote: "Had I permitted myself any innovation on the original term, it would have been to convert it to Australia."

BASS STRAIT?

Flinders wrote Bass a letter in 1800 that lay undiscovered until 1998. It contained the following lines:

> There was a time, when I was so completely wrapped up in you, that no conversation but yours could give me any degree of pleasure; your footsteps on the quarterdeck over my head, took me from my book, and brought me upon deck to walk with you ... and yet it is not clear to me that I love you entirely; at least my affection for Wiles reaches farther into my heart — I would take him into the same skin as me!

This tender missive was never received by Bass, who had left his London home (like Flinders, after just three months of marriage) to drown off the South American coast. The letter was opened and read by the new Mrs Bass, who scrawled a note to her husband on its envelope:

> This George is written by a Man that bears a bad Character no one has seen this letter but I could tell you many things that make me dislike him.

The letter and the somewhat alarmed response of Mrs Bass have led to speculation that Flinders, in the sailing vernacular of his age, puffed with the southerly wind.

Yet many historians insist that Flinders's marriage and venereal disease prove that he was straight (gay men clearly don't marry women or get the clap, and bisexuality doesn't even bear thinking about). They contend that the letter was an example of "romantic friendship" of the kind experienced by Shakespeare and his Fair Youth, diggers in the trenches of Gallipoli (none of whom could possibly have been gay[7][8]), and Matt Damon and Ben Affleck. They would be prepared to reconsider their position if presented with sufficient historical proof to the contrary – for example, a portrait of Bass and Flinders in a hot tub, signed by both explorers and witnessed by Governor Hunter.

This sort of proof is hard to come by. Homosexual activity was not uncommon at the turn of the nineteenth century, particularly in the Royal Navy, but it was extremely dangerous for a young sailor to come out of Davy Jones's Locker.

Buggery was, in Flinders's day, the crime that dare not speak its name.[9] Sir William Blackstone, England's greatest eighteenth-century jurisprudist (and prudist generally), wrote in his *Commentaries on the Laws of England*:

> I will not act so disagreeable a part, to my readers as well as myself, as to dwell any longer upon a subject, the very mention of which is a disgrace to human nature. It will be more eligible to imitate in this respect the delicacy of our English

---

7   Not even a little bit.

8   The rumours about Simpson and his donkey are also untrue.

9   Henry VIII was prepared to speak it when he passed the 1533 *Buggerie Acte* (formally "*An Acte for the punysshement of the vice of Buggerie*"). The *Buggery Act* remained largely unchanged until 1828 (although someone ran a spellcheck) and buggery remained a capital offence in Britain until 1861 (and until as late as 1887 in the Australian colonies).

law, which treats it, in its very indictments, as a crime not fit
to be named ...

The death penalty for the unnameable crime was rigor-
ously enforced, while those convicted of the lesser crimes of
attempted no-namery or being a bit suss were punished with
time in the pillory (similar to the stocks). This was often a
de facto death sentence, as the mob would pelt them with
any ready-to-hand heavy objects.

Jeremy Bentham, the guy who devised disciplinary prisons and the wonderful whipping machine, wrote *Offences
Against One's Self* in 1785. In it, Bentham argued that homo-
sexuality, although involving "irregularities of the venereal
appetite", was essentially a private matter that didn't hurt
anyone, and that Britain should therefore stop hanging gay
people. However, this view was so radical that Bentham
buried the essay in his sock draw and it remained unpub-
lished until 1931.

The death of Viscount Castlereagh, the British secretary
of state for war and the colonies at the time of the Rum
Rebellion, illustrates the difficulty of being a gay Georgian.
In 1822, Castlereagh, then leader of the House of Commons,
advised King George IV that he was being blackmailed for
homosexual acts, confessing, "I am accused of the same
crime as the Bishop of Clogher." [10] The King advised him
to consult a physician. Instead, Castlereagh returned to his

---

10   The Bishop of Clogher, the suggestively named Percy Jocelyn (the cards were
     really stacked against him), was found with a naked Grenadier Guardsman in
     the backroom of a Westminster pub earlier in 1822. He skipped bail, assumed
     the name Thomas Wilson, and went to work as a butler in Scotland, a land
     where a man might wear a skirt with pride.

FIG. 8: PROOF.

estate and cut his throat with a letter opener. His funeral procession was jeered along its whole route. [11]

---

[11] Lord Byron penned the following touching obituary to Castlereagh:

> *Posterity will ne'er survey*
> *A nobler grave than this:*
> *Here lie the bones of Castlereagh:*
> *Stop, traveller, and piss.*

So, were Bass and Flinders more than "just good sailing buddies"? There is certainly some circumstantial evidence that Flinders sailed counter-clockwise:

1. Flinders was in the Royal Navy.
2. He chose to emigrate to a place with the world's highest male–female ratio and a flexible approach to issues of conventional morality.
3. He enjoyed intimate sailing trips and repeatedly exploring the same place with a fellow traveller.
4. He had a small animal companion.
5. He ran away from his wife as soon as was decently practicable.
6. He played the flute.
7. He was a hairdresser.
8. His favourite book was about a chap marooned on an island with only an obliging Man Friday for company.
9. His charting of Tasmania gave the atlas its only pink triangle.

Gay, straight or somewhere in between, Matthew Flinders sits atop the pantheon of true-blue Aussie heroes.

THE PASSING OF THE BATON

The forty-year-old Flinders, ravaged by the gravelly, lapsed into a coma and died on 19 July 1814, the day after his book was published. He didn't get to see his continent renamed. But on 12 December 1817, the governor of New South Wales recommended that Britain adopt the name Australia. That governor's name was Lachlan Macquarie.

9

The Great
Economiser

My riches a' 's my penny-fee,
An' I maun guide it cannie, O

My Nannie, O,
Robert Burns, 1783

HAE YE A SPARE PENNY?

L ACHLAN MACQUARIE WAS A SCOTSMAN TO HIS
bootstraps – which, he'd be proud to let you know,
he'd bought for an absolute bargain at an Edinburgh
thrift store. He was cousin to the ancient chieftain of clan
MacQuarrie, nephew to the Laird of Lochbuy, and a proud
son of Ulva.

Ulva, a tiny windswept speck in the North Atlantic, was
noted only for its kelp industry and, according to Dr Samuel
Johnson, for being the last place in Britain where the local
lord still claimed the feudal right to bed a bride on her wedding night – although Johnson acknowledged that Auld

MacQuarrie was prepared to break with tradition if the groom gifted him a sheep.[1]

Most of the Ulbhachs, as the island's natives were known, aspired to nothing more than a good seaweed harvest and marriage to a cousin who had not been too badly scarred by the pox.[2] But young Lachlan dreamed of restoring the name and fortune of his once mighty clan.

In 1746, sixteen years before Lachlan's birth, the English had thrashed the Highland clans at the Battle of Culloden and stripped the MacQuarries of most of their lands, their kilts[3] and their sporrans.[4] Three decades later, the 63-year-old clan chief's finances were so dire that he was forced to join the British Army and travel across the Atlantic to fight Americans.

Fourteen-year-old Lachlan also enlisted and travelled to Canada, the United States and Jamaica without getting to fight anyone, which was a profound disappointment to him. Army wages were poor and a soldier could only secure

---

1   Sheep are highly valued in Scotland as they are the principal ingredient of haggis, a hideous boiled sausage made from sheep offal and oatmeal, encased in a sheep's stomach. This unspeakably vile concoction became the national dish of Scotland following the publication of Robert Burns's *Address to a Haggis* in 1787, but has since been supplanted by the deep-fried Mars Bar.

2   The Ulbhachs' passion for inbreeding may explain the "forlorn and helpless situation" of Donald Macquarie, Lachlan's idiot brother.

3   The British Parliament passed a law in 1747 banning Highlanders from wearing kilts and other traditional dress outside the British army, with Scots-dressing carrying a penalty of seven years' transportation. This law was repealed in 1782 because the Americans refused to accept further deliveries of angry skirt-wearing rangas.

4   The sporran is a furry pouch that hangs at the front of a Scotsman's pocketless kilt. Scotsmen use their sporrans to store hipflasks, knuckle-dusters and any small denomination coins they have not yet had the opportunity to bury in their backyards.

his fortune by looting the towns of the defeated foe. It was the spoils of war that attracted hordes of Scotsmen to join the British Army, as fighting and stealing were etched onto the DNA of every man born north of Hadrian's Wall.

Macquarie was offered another opportunity to fight and steal from foreigners in 1787, this time in India. But first he had to buy a lieutenancy and pay fifteen men to fight and steal under him. This would require him to go into debt, which was the worst four-letter word in his vocabulary. Macquarie, like most Scots, knew the value of a penny. His diaries record in excruciatingly detail the prices of goods purchased throughout his life.[5] But the young Scot calculated that the gold and gems he would liberate from the recalcitrant maharajas of the Orient would prove his commission a canny investment.

And so we find the 25-year-old Macquarie striding through the misty Highlands in search of fifteen brave and reasonably priced countrymen prepared to join him in the heat and dust of India.

HAE TE A SPARE RUPEE?

Bombay proved a disappointment. Macquarie had been there for three years and hadn't been allowed to fight or

---

5   The thriftiness of Scots is well recognised in the commercial world. McFrugal is Scotland's most popular online hardware chain, while Scotch tape received its name after a client of the 3M company criticised the lack of adhesive in the middle of the tape and told a salesman to take the product back to his "Scotch bosses". 3M embraced the Scotch name because economising was regarded as a virtue during the Great Depression era in which the tape was invented.

steal from anyone. He finally got his chance in 1791 against Tipu Saib, the Sultan of Mysore. During the campaign, Macquarie took to the field with six bullocks, ten servants, eight dozen bottles of brandy and Madeira, and "a quantity of gin". This was travelling light by Indian Army standards – some officers campaigned with over forty servants.

The overburdened soldiers were soon bogged down in monsoonal rains and bombarded by the iron-cased rockets recently invented by the Mysoreans. By the time they reached Tipu's stronghold, they were so wet and shell-shocked that they retreated without firing a shot. Macquarie was laid low with dysentery and malaria and Indians looted most of his possessions on the long journey back to barracks. War had not lived up to expectations.

Having failed to make his fortune through military endeavour, Macquarie threw himself into Bombay's social circuit of balls and music parties and fell in love with Miss Jane Jarvis and her inheritance. Jane was the daughter of a Jamaican plantation owner and, like many young women of sufficient means and insufficient breeding, had travelled to India in the hope of securing a suitable boy from among the ranks of Britain's most eligible looters.

Macquarie was determined to impress Jane with his discipline, which one of his diary entries defined as getting dressed by half-past two in the afternoon, drinking no more than twelve glasses of wine and one strong beer a night, and only consuming malt liquor during daylight hours.

Macquarie and Jane married, but only after Macquarie signed a legal agreement confirming that he would not make use of her money. He soon found matrimony an uneconomic proposition. He had to buy new china and linen, decorated fans, parasols, songbirds, picnic baskets, embroidery patterns, pianoforte sheet music, smelling salts and other feminine necessities. Married officers were also expected to invite the single chaps around for Friday drinks.[6] Macquarie, who was spending 800 rupees for every 500 he earned, soon fell out with his in-laws over a "misunderstanding", which was Macquarie-speak for being caught trying to draw down on Jane's inheritance.

The grafting Highlander found the answer to his financial problems when he was appointed regimental paymaster. He arranged to receive the funds for the regiment's wages before his men were due to be paid, and invested it for his own benefit. He also attempted to rebuild the fortunes of the Macquarie clan by sponsoring fake army commissions and getting relatives as young as five to change their names to match those of the fictional officers. This enabled his kinsmen to draw military pay while happily harvesting seaweed thousands of miles away from the nearest battlefield.

Macquarie's career was progressing nicely. He'd led the British Army into the Dutch settlement of Cochin and kicked the tulip-growers out of Ceylon. He was devastated by his wife's death in 1796, but the cloud of her passing had a sterling-silver lining: a £6,000 inheritance.

Macquarie was now posted to fight Napoleon in Egypt. The campaign was almost over when he arrived, but he stayed long enough to learn to ride a camel and contract syphilis.

---

6   After one such session, Macquarie's shaky diary entry read, "No beer for three months."

He returned to Britain in 1803 with the rank of major, a fortune of £20,000, and George Jarvis, an Indian slave boy he had purchased for 85 rupees and given a new name for free. George would stay by Macquarie's side for the rest of his life.

Macquarie hoped never to see a samosa again. He would return to the sweet haggis of his youth, haggle over the price of a modest estate on the Isle of Mull, and spend the remainder of his days burying his money on its grounds. But reality and the taxman would intrude to shatter this Highland idyll.

AN ECONOMY WITH THE TRUTH

Within months of his return, Macquarie was forced to part with twelve guineas for an operation "of a very delicate nature". The Cairo Clap was playing havoc with his waterworks and Macquarie required ongoing treatment, which involved periodically dipping the affected region into a dish of liquid mercury.[7]

Macquarie was also having trouble with tax, in that he was being asked to pay it. He successfully claimed that £3,000 worth of shares he owned were the property of his brother and that £1,000 found in his house belonged to an unusually wealthy servant. Emboldened by these victories[8]

---

7   This highly toxic metal remained the principal treatment for syphilis until the invention of antibiotics, giving rise to the saying, "One night with Venus and a lifetime with Mercury." Mercury treatment for venereal disease commonly resulted in tooth loss, skin lesions, spongy bones, neurological damage and/or dropping dead from mercury poisoning.

8   Macquarie literally got off "scot-free". The scot was a thirteenth-century tax levied to support the poor and the term scot-free was used to describe successful tax evasion.

over the taxman, Macquarie embarked on one fraud too many.

Macquarie lobbied for the "wonderfully stout and active" Auld MacQuarrie to be commissioned an officer of the Horse Guards. He proposed that the sprightly chieftain, just a few months shy of his ninetieth birthday, be given full pay while being granted permanent leave from sitting on a horse or guarding anything. This arrangement was so unusual that it was drawn to the attention of the Duke of York, the British Army's commander-in-chief. After a bit of digging, the duke found he had also been paying the Horse Guard salaries of two of Macquarie's prepubescent kinsmen.[9]

The duke demanded that Macquarie produce these mysterious officers, who had never turned up for duty. Macquarie regretfully declined on the grounds that they had just sailed for Jamaica to manage a sugar plantation. The duke suggested Macquarie was being economical with the truth and Macquarie finally admitted that the officers were attending a primary school just down the road. With breathtaking audacity, he then asked the duke to keep them on full pay while they completed their schooling. The furious duke kicked the boys out of the army and punished Macquarie by booking him another passage to India.

On the night before he left, Macquarie performed the traditional Ulbhach ritual of asking for his cousin's hand in marriage. Elizabeth Campbell, Macquarie's second cousin once removed and sister to his aunt by marriage,

---

9   HRH Prince Frederick was the Grand Old Duke of York of nursery rhyme
      fame. He had 10,000 men and two small Scottish boys.

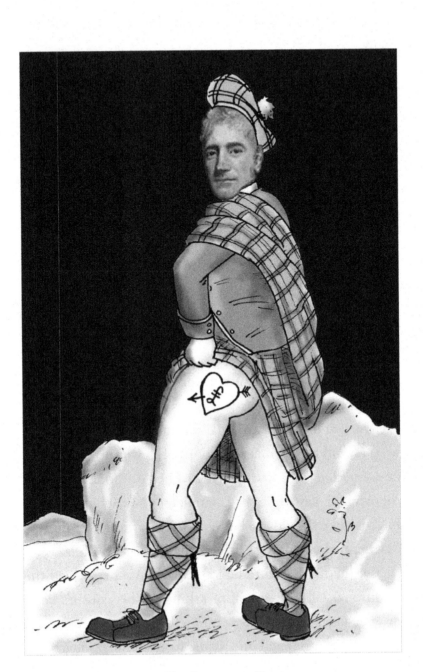

FIG. 9: THE EDINBURGH TATTOO.

was a sensible girl with a keen interest in gardening and architecture. Her practical nature appealed to Macquarie. Although he initially felt no passion for her, he was satisfied he'd found a companion who could keep house and, with any luck, mow his lawn and build him a gazebo.

Sadly, the only fighting Macquarie saw during the following two years in India was with the army's paymaster, who objected to meeting his extravagant liquor bills. He married Elizabeth upon his return and took command of the Black Watch, a regiment of Scotland's most vicious and bloodthirsty looters. The Watch was to travel to New South Wales to replace the disgraced Rum Corps and an army man was to be appointed governor, given the colony's previous naval rulers had failed to command the loyalty of their troops.

The governorship was given to Major-General Miles Nightingall, who immediately developed a mysterious arthritis of the wrist that prevented him from travelling. Nightingall sat around for months until he was told he didn't have to sail for Sydney if he didn't want to, at which time his wrist miraculously recovered and accepted a posting more to its liking in Spain. Macquarie wrote to Lord Castlereagh, the colonial secretary, suggesting that his wrist was up to governing New South Wales. Much to everybody's surprise, Castlereagh gave him the job.

Macquarie was an unusual choice. At forty-seven, he was the oldest lieutenant-colonel in the army. He'd been caught arranging dodgy commissions and lying to the royal family. He was in poor health, with his skin yellowed from malaria and a liver that had spent decades being kicked by Johnny Walker. His face and limbs were blotched from the curative acids he applied to his syphilitic lesions and years of bathing "Wee Mister Mac" in mercury had left him with a disconcerting neurological twitch.

Macquarie was appointed because most competent men of rank didn't want to live with habitual criminals, mutinous soldiers and naked savages in a far-flung land that had destroyed the career of every governor since Phillip. And Britannia had her hands full with Frenchmen who'd learned to fight and Americans who'd decided they wanted to own Canada after all. New South Wales was nothing more than the echo of an afterthought in the distracted mind of Mother Britain.

MOPPING UP SPILT RUM

Macquarie was sworn in on 1 January 1810, a new governor for a new decade. He had orders to restore Bligh as governor for a day and then send him packing. But the Bastard was nowhere to be found. Bligh, who'd been released after promising to return to England, had instead seized the ship that was to take him home and sailed for Van Diemen's Land, demanding that the Vandemonians invade New South Wales on his behalf.

The Vandemonians were having none of it and Bligh offended lieutenant-governor David Collins by making snide comments about his pregnant convict mistress. Collins said of his unwelcome guest, "God knows I never had any malice in my heart until I came into contact with this detestable brute."

Bligh returned to his ship in a sulk and spent the next six months blockading Hobart. Collins ordered his people to fire on the deranged ex-governor if he attempted land-fall. Bligh ran out of supplies and once again found himself starving at sea. He survived by letting ships through his blockade if their captains gave him a biscuit.

Back in Sydney, Macquarie told the remaining rebels that they'd been very naughty and asked them not to rebel again. George Johnston had returned to Britain to be court-martialled for treason and Macarthur had also fled New South Wales following a duel with Lieutenant-Colonel Foveaux, the officer tasked with restoring order after the rebellion. As a gesture of reconciliation, the new governor dug deep into the Australian zeitgeist, unearth-ing a powerful mortar to bind the fractious colonists together. Sport.

Macquarie noticed that settlers and convicts gathered together on Sydney's streets to enjoy horse races, weighted footraces[10], fist fights, dog fights, cock fights and any other sort of fight. Like the emperors of ancient Rome, with whom his critics later compared him, Macquarie cemented his rule with bread and circuses. He set aside a section of the Commons for the "recreation and amusement of the

---

10   William Francis King, known as the Flying Pieman, was Australia's greatest ever weight-racer. He made a living betting on himself in races against other competitors or in outlandish challenges against the clock, sometimes demanding that he be horsewhipped to maximise his performance. He walked from Campbelltown to Sydney in nine hours carrying a 32-kilogram dog and from Sydney to Parramatta in seven hours carrying a 36-kilogram goat. He later ran a mile, walked a mile, pushed a wheelbarrow a half-mile, dragged a fat lady in a carriage a half-mile, walked backwards a half-mile and leapt over fifty stones set a yard apart, all in less than ninety minutes. King's feats of endurance became so well known that nobody was prepared to bet against him. Deprived of his income and clearly as mad as a cut snake, he died penniless in Liverpool Asylum.

inhabitants of the town" and named it Hyde Park, holding Australia's first officially sanctioned horse races there two days later. The 1810 racing carnival lasted three days and the whole town came out to gamble, drink and fight. Macquarie soon held another fair at which "ladies raced in sacks for a cheese" and gentleman came to bet on them and have a good laugh.

Macquarie's attempts to reconcile the colony's hostile factions were temporarily derailed when Bligh and his daughter returned. The crowd would hoot and jeer at the ex-governor as he scuttled to Government House to present his increasingly shrill demands that Macquarie exact vengeance on those who had brought him down. For four months Macquarie politely ignored Bligh's tantrums, reporting to his non-idiot brother, Charles:

> He certainly is a most disagreeable Person to have any dealings, or Publick business to transact with ... he is a very improper Person to be employed in any situation of Trust or Command and he is certainly generally detested by high, low, rich and poor ...

Mary, who had spent the last two years locked up in Government House and starving off the coast of Tasmania, hastily married the colony's new lieutenant-governor, Maurice O'Connell. Bligh, devastated by this most personal of mutinies, sailed home without his beloved daughter. He was accompanied by Atkins, Paterson and many other powerful men of the colony, as well as the soldiers of the Corps that had deposed him. This made for strained after-dinner conversation during the five-month voyage.

The British didn't know what to do with Bligh, so they made him an admiral. The most divisive character in Australia's short history drew his last breath in 1817, a complete and utter Bastard to the end.

THE SCUM ALSO RISES

The officers of the Corps had been the administrative backbone of the colony. Their departure left a vacuum that the Black Watch couldn't fill. This meant that the new governor was forced to make appointments that his predecessors would have considered ... distasteful.

D'Arcy Wentworth was the greatest beneficiary of this new order. Macquarie confirmed D'Arcy's appointment as the colony's principal surgeon and made him a justice of the peace, magistrate, member of the Governor's Court, commissioner of police, treasurer of the Police Fund, and turnpike commissioner.[11] D'Arcy had more hats than a geriatric milliner. He also had a chequered past.

D'Arcy was born of noble stock, a distant cousin to Charles Watson-Wentworth, a two-time British prime minister whose nephew, Earl Fitzwilliam, sponsored D'Arcy's entrée into London society. But D'Arcy was the son of a publican from the stunted Irish branch of the Wentworth family tree and his surgeon's income prevented him from keeping up with the St-Johnses. Determined to maintain a gentleman's

---

11 Macquarie's first big public works project was the Sydney to Parramatta turnpike (toll road). He was the first New South Wales governor to believe in infrastructure, but he also believed in other people paying for it. Tolls were a typical Scots solution.

lifestyle, D'Arcy took on a second job and became Britain's most notorious surgeon-highwayman. [12]

D'Arcy was charged with four armed robberies between 1787 and 1789. On one occasion, he was caught carrying a pistol and black silk mask near the scene of a hold-up. On another, he left a stolen watch in court. Slips of this kind normally guaranteed the noose, but D'Arcy's Irish charm and family connections resulted in a series of stunning acquittals.

The Times's regular articles on the escapades of "the famous D'Arcy Wentworth" mortified Fitzwilliam, who encouraged his kinsman to book a ticket to Sydney before a judge did it for him. D'Arcy, who emigrated with the Second Fleet, was the first of many black sheep sent to Australia by embarrassed relatives.

D'Arcy worked as a doctor and convict supervisor, but Fitzwilliam's grudging assistance enabled him to start an import business and buy up farmland. The amiable surgeon was soon one of the wealthiest men in the colony. He was well liked, but his colourful history meant he would never be entirely trusted by the colony's elite.

Macquarie, however, trusted D'Arcy absolutely. He believed that a man should not be judged for his past actions, but for his recent conduct. He also believed that a man should not be judged when he is responsible for regularly cauterising one's recurring genital ulcers with a red-hot wire.

D'Arcy was not the only of Macquarie's appointments to raise eyebrows. The madman was giving plum jobs to

---

12   Being a surgeon didn't carry the same cachet it does now. Surgeons doubled as barbers until 1745 and, by D'Arcy's time, were regarded as little more than hairdressers with ambition and extra-large scissors.

ex-convicts! Simeon Lord and Andrew Thompson, onetime cloth thieves, were appointed turnpike commissioners alongside D'Arcy and, to the settlers' horror, were elevated to the Magistracy, where they passed judgement on those for whom they had previously laboured.

Later, Macquarie explained his approach to ex-convicts (known as "emancipists") thus: "My principle is, that when once a man is free, his former state should no longer be remembered, or allowed to act against him." His critics, however, believed that the convict stain could never be washed away. As far as they were concerned, the inmates were taking over the asylum.

CURRENCY LADS

Macquarie also provided opportunities to those born within the colony. Most of his countrymen regarded the native-born as the depraved spawn of criminal degenerates, prone to idleness, compulsive drinking and poor personal hygiene.

The native-born were actually far healthier than their British counterparts, having enjoyed a childhood free of being stuffed up chimneys or down coalmines. They enjoyed full employment and shorter working hours than British labourers and, even when food was scarce, never had to resort to dead rats, bark or lumps of coal, those staples of working-class English cuisine.

The first colonial teenagers rejected their parents' values, as teenagers have done ever since Cain and Abel decided to get away from all that hippy nature stuff. They were sober, industrious and, if truth be told, not much fun. They laboured uncomplainingly in the sun, exercised in the fresh air, swam in the sea and were, on average, six inches taller than the malnourished British stock from which they had sprung. Within a single generation, the Artful Dodger had transformed into Chesty Bond.

Even so, most of these mild colonial boys were convinced of their inferiority. Young Hamilton Hume, a Parramatta-born protégé of Macquarie, expressed hope that he might one day be trusted to do some exploring, "altho' an Australian". The first generation of nouveau-Australians had chips on their shoulders and, what's more, they believed British chips were better. They had just invented the cultural cringe.

The native-born were known as "currency" after the banknotes that lacked the intrinsic value of the "sterling", the pound of silver that served as the British monetary standard and lent its name to the British-born colonists. [13] While many native-born wore the currency tag with a sense of shame, a few, like William Charles Wentworth, adopted it as a badge of honour.

William was the eldest son of Catherine Crowley, D'Arcy's seventeen-year-old convict mistress. The timing of his birth suggests he was the product of a pre-D'Arcy dalliance, but D'Arcy adopted William upon Catherine's untimely death and sent him to England for a classical education. Keen-minded but lazy, William spent his school days writing poetry, drinking port and blowing his

---

13   Macquarie's inner Scot was thrilled to have arrived in a land where the people named themselves after money.

allowance on lottery tickets. He was unable to get a job in England, which he attributed to anti-colonial prejudice and others attributed to his being an insufferable smart-arse. Dispirited, he returned to the colony with no skills beyond being able to order a drink and place a bet in Latin, Ancient Greek and haiku.

William was a lump of a lad, with coarse features and an unkempt shock of ginger hair. His dishevelled look was complemented by a cast eye that stared disconcertingly over the shoulder of whomever he happened to be shouting at. William was an enthusiastic shouter, with a voice like treacle being poured down a foghorn. He would use this formidable instrument to harangue any person foolish enough to disagree with him, concluding each outburst by saying something incomprehensible, although obviously very clever, in Latin – or by delivering a withering put-down in flawless iambic pentameter.

Macquarie was impressed by William's shouting skills and appointed him acting provost marshal, placing him in charge of the colony's public meetings and hanging roster. William, the first native-born to be appointed to a senior position in the colony, would devote his life to cutting Australia loose from the apron-strings of Mother Britain.

THERE'S SOMETHING ABOUT MARY

Macquarie also encouraged women to participate in public life, starting in his own home. Elizabeth Macquarie oversaw the transformation of Sydney's rugged Domain into sculptured parkland, with the harbour-view sandstone bench she commissioned still known as Mrs Macquarie's Chair. She also introduced hay-making to the colony and was a director of the Bank of New South Wales.

Australian women had opportunities beyond those afforded to their British sisters. This was, in large part, a product of the law of supply and demand. Women were in short supply and high demand, enabling them to negoti- ate a better life for themselves. They were able to choose from an increasingly desperate line-up of prospective suit- ors and, if a partner didn't come up to scratch, he could be traded in for a better and wealthier model. [14]

Back in the Old Dart, everything a woman owned passed to her husband upon marriage. In the colony, a convict couldn't own land or trading licences so, where a freewoman was married to a convict, she owned all such property. Convict men were also commonly assigned as servants to their free wives. If a man in such a situation stayed out late with his mates or forgot to put the privy seat down, the missus could discharge him from her service and send him to the chain gang.

Men on the frontier sometimes returned to Britain, leaving their wives or mistresses in charge of their Aus- tralian affairs. Elizabeth Macarthur, for example, took on the family's pastoral concerns in John's absence. A dead or absent partner, and a dearth of local male relatives, often

---

14   The socio-economic consequences of the colonial gender differential are explained by the following econometric formula:

$$\frac{9\male\pounds}{\female} = 5\male\pounds + \frac{\male\pounds}{\male\pounds} + \frac{\male\pounds}{\text{🐖}} + \frac{\female\pounds}{\male}$$

conspired to leave substantial business interests in the hands of colonial women.

Of course, colonial women still did it pretty tough. In 1811, a Sydney man was lashed for putting a halter around his wife's neck and selling her at market for £16. But on the bright side, a wife seller in Britain might escape punishment altogether and the market value of a second-hand spouse was considerably less.[15] Things were definitely looking up for Australian women.

Nobody embodies female colonial opportunity more than Mary Reibey. The po-faced grandmother on our $20 note was Australia's first cross-dressing, horse-thieving, seal-clubbing convict entrepreneur and standover woman.

Thirteen-year-old Mary was a middle-class girl who was, as the English would say, "high-spirited" and, as we Australians would say, "a little shit". She eloped with another girl, dressed as a boy, assumed the name James Burrow, stole a horse and was sentenced to death. James went through the courts and spent months in a crowded cell without anyone realising he was a she. After the sentence was commuted, her gender was revealed during the compulsory pre-transportation bath and an appeal was lodged for her pardon. The appeal fell on deaf ears. Magistrates hated drag kings even more than they hated horse thieves and Mary was lucky to escape to New South Wales with her life.[16]

---

15   *The Times* later reported that a man took his haltered wife to Axbridge market and sold her for a shilling. The Sydney spouse was worth an incredible 320 times the value of her English counterpart. Australian women should be proud of this difference in the used-wife exchange rate.

16   British magistrates ordered a number of women executed for impersonating

At age seventeen, Mary married Thomas Reibey, a junior East India Company officer. When Thomas died young, Mary inherited his extensive pastoral, hotel, shipping and sealing concerns. She expanded her empire through canny investments and a single-mindedly vicious approach to anyone who owed her money, all the while caring for seven children. Despite being convicted of beating a debtor like he was her red-headed stepson, Mary remained a Macquarie favourite and prospered under his rule, helping him establish the Bank of New South Wales and leasing him her house to serve as its first branch.

Macquarie's willingness to work with black sheep, ex-cons, the native-born, women and other undesirables has led to him being viewed as a champion of Australian democracy, a notion that would have made him furious. Macquarie wrote of his implacable hatred of the "infernal and destructive principles of Democracy", which he believed to be decadently Greek, unfashionably French and dangerously American.

Macquarie didn't have a democratic bone in his body. He was an equal-opportunity autocrat who didn't mind who you were, what you'd done or whom you'd done it to, as long as you obeyed his commands and didn't cost him money.

Ah, money ...

That was still proving to be a bit of a problem.

---

men, in accordance with Deuteronomy 22:5: "The woman shall not wear that which pertaineth unto a man, neither shall a man put on a woman's garment: for all that do so are abomination unto the LORD thy God." The sexist British legal system did not similarly punish cross-dressing men, much to the relief of Scotsmen and generations of Tory MPs.

10

I think I'll call it Macquarie

Or maybe Lachlan ...
Lachlan's a good name too.

Governor Lachlan Macquarie,
1810, 1811, 1812, 1813, 1814, 1815,
1816, 1817, 1818, 1819, 1820, 1821

THE HOLY DOLLAR

RUM WAS STILL THE COLONY'S FAVOURED CURRENCY when Lachlan Macquarie was decanted from his vessel after the seven-month journey from Portsmouth. Lord Castlereagh, the colonial secretary, had ordered the new governor to "prohibit the Use of Spirituous Liquors", but he may as well have told the notoriously tight Scot to burn thousands of pounds and sprinkle the ashes in Botany Bay.

Rum was both an alcoholic drink and money, which were Macquarie's two favourite things – there was no way he'd be getting rid of it. Instead, he distributed lucrative liquor licenses to his allies and recommended that Britain approve the unlimited importation of alcohol, with a steep rise in import duties. This would fill his coffers while buying the continued loyalty of his supporters.

Meanwhile, convicts were dying in an inefficient and disorderly manner. They were dying in their homes. They were dying in the fields. They were dying in pubs, shops, churches and alleyways. The only place they weren't dying was the hospital. This was not the hospital's fault. It was an absolute death-trap, complete with termite-infested walls, streams of raw sewage, and heavily tattooed male nurses whose bedside manners would have been called into question if the hospital had had any beds.

Macquarie, who had spent much of his life having unpleasant things done to his sporran-region, was a firm believer in quality healthcare. He wanted to build a hospital that people would be happy to be seen dead in, but simply couldn't afford it. Then one of the few pennies in the colony dropped. He would build the grandest hospital the world had ever seen. And he would build it with rum.

Macquarie signed a contract with D'Arcy Wentworth and two local entrepreneurs. They would build him a vast hospital with lots of ornamental pillars and ostentatious latticework, in accordance with the eccentric designs of an unknown architect whom many believe to have been Mrs Macquarie. He would give them eighty oxen, the use of twenty draught bullocks and twenty convict labourers, and the exclusive right to import 60,000 gallons of rum over the next three years. D'Arcy and his friends believed

Macquarie was handing them the entire colonial economy on a big, shiny platter.

But the builders had ignored the fine print. "Exclusive" didn't include shipments of rum that had already been approved and, unbeknownst to the colonists, Britain had endorsed Macquarie's proposal to allow unlimited liquor into the colony. A merchant fleet was already on its way, carrying enough booze to knock out Keith Richards (i.e. 76,000 gallons).

Macquarie also retained the right to import "what Government may deem necessary for its own use and occasions". He deemed away like there was no tomorrow, paying convicts in rum for government work. Over 120,000 gallons entered the colony, eroding the value of the hospitallers' investment. They had learned an important lesson – never play Monopoly with a Scot.

Macquarie had invested £4,200 worth of cows and convicts in the project and had taken £9,000 in spirit duties and a £40,000 hospital from the builders. This was Scottish financial management at its best. Macquarie boasted to Lord Liverpool, who had replaced Castlereagh, of his success in pulling off a public–private partnership in which the public hadn't had their privates completely screwed.

Liverpool was livid. Not only had Macquarie squandered thousands of pounds on sick criminals, but funding the project with spirits was an "embarrassment". Liverpool accused Macquarie of wasting money, which was the greatest insult that could be levelled at a Scot. The shattered governor assured Liverpool that there had never been "a

greater economist in every branch of public expenditure"
than his niggardly self.

The Rum Hospital, as it was known, received its first
patient six years after it was commissioned. Its mysterious
architect had forgotten to include any toilets, so bedpans
accumulated until the nurse-warders opened the windows to slop their contents onto the ground below (the
windows were opened infrequently because patients kept
trying to escape out of them). Food was prepared in the
crowded wards because the hospital's kitchen was being
used as a morgue, with smoke and grease from the roar-
ing cookfires combining with the scent of the overflowing
bedpans to create a toxic miasma. Syphilis was rife, with
venereal patients locked in a storeroom and the doors of
the male and female wards bolted from the outside in a
futile attempt to prevent patients from having sex. Nurses
would throw warm meat at the ill, rather than serve it
on a plate, which D'Arcy explained was to protect them
from contagion. Medicine, bandages and stockings were
in short supply, as hospital staff stole them to sell on the
black market.

The hospital was colloquially known as the Sydney
Slaughterhouse. Its interior was reminiscent of something
painted by Hieronymus Bosch on one of his really bad days,
but it looked great from Macquarie Street, as the governor
had indulgently named the new boulevard that ran past the
hospital's majestically porticoed entrance.

It seems somehow fitting that this building, shiny on
the outside, but rotten at its core, with its disease, noxious
vapours, illicit intercourse, petty theft, hurled food and

excrement, and its inmates shielded from public view, now serves as New South Wales's Parliament House.

Despite his love of rum, Macquarie knew the colony could not continue to run on a currency prone to spillage and evaporation. In 1813, he imported 40,000 Spanish dollars and gave them to William Henshall, a convicted coiner, with instructions to cut the centre out of each coin. Henshall established Australia's first coining mint and produced a donut-shaped coin, known as the holey dollar, which was issued as the colony's principal currency. The disc removed from the dollar's centre, known as the dump, entered circulation as a small-denomination coin. Macquarie, in a moment of Scottish fiscal genius, declared that the two new coins would have a combined value of one-and-a-quarter dollars, generating a tidy profit for his government. [1]

Now that people had cold hard cash, they needed somewhere to put it. In 1817, Macquarie encouraged D'Arcy and others, mostly emancipists, to establish the Bank of New South Wales, Australia's first public company. The bank was to accept deposits, make loans and print the colony's first banknotes. [2] Most of the gentlemen of the anti-emancipist

---

1   Macquarie's creative accounting inspired Australia's largest merchant-bank, Macquarie Bank, to adopt his name and take the holey dollar as its logo. The bank, like its namesake, is famed for its money-spinning tollroads and other infrastructure projects.

2   In the early nineteenth century, most banknotes were issued by banks, rather than the state. In 1826, the British Parliament introduced laws to prevent banks from issuing notes valued at less than £5. This outraged the Scots, who could not dream of ever parting with so large a sum, and Scotland's greatest novelist, Sir Walter Scott, mounted a successful campaign to save the Scottish £1 note. Three private Scottish banks continue to issue their own banknotes

"exclusive" faction, who had previously loaned money at exorbitant rates, boycotted the bank.

The bank had teething problems. D'Arcy, who played a key role in setting its interest rates, undercut those rates through a dodgy loan agency he'd established. Directors were given banknotes to sign, some of which were never seen again. Francis Williams, an early manager, was regularly taken out to a club, plied with alcohol and then asked to issue loans without security. It was finally discovered that Williams had given away £12,000 of the bank's £12,600 starting capital and had attempted to cover up the bank's impending insolvency by entering non-existent deposits in its books.

But the bank survived and eventually thrived, eroding the financial services monopoly of the exclusive class and forever changing the way business was done in the colony. The real Macquarie Bank, once disparagingly referred to as "the convicts' bank", is now known as Westpac.

MACQUARIE, MACQUARIE, MACQUARIE

At the end of Bligh's rule, the colony comprised land within a day's ride of Sydney and the convict hellholes of Newcastle and Van Diemen's Land.[3] Macquarie wanted to upsize his little corner of empire, so he traipsed around the countryside

---

to this day and Scott's miserly victory continues to be celebrated by the Bank of Scotland, which includes Scott's portrait on all of its banknotes.

3   Readers who are interested in banjo playing, cannibalism and genocide will be able to learn all about Tasmania in the second volume of *The Unauthorised History of Australia*.

founding new settlements and naming prominent landmarks after himself or, when feeling sentimental, after his wife.

The grandest street in every new town was named Macquarie Street and the governor soon bestowed his name on rivers, hills, falls, fields, plains, a pass, an island, a mountain, a tower, a fort and a port. The kilt-clad egomaniac also named his child after himself, with young Lachlan Macquarie born during a dinner party for the colony's officers, who politely ignored Mrs Macquarie's screams as they passed the port.

Macquarie liked to lead grand exploration parties, a hangover from his Indian Army days. He explored the Hunter Valley with over fifty companions, including a band of musicians. He explored long and he explored hard, which was very tiring for his entourage, particularly the double bass player.

The impenetrable Blue Mountains, with majestic peaks approaching 4,000 feet, kept the secrets of the vast western inland locked away and hidden from all.[4] Then, in 1813, William Wentworth decided to pop over the ranges to see what was on the other side. His exploring buddies were Gregory Blaxland, one of the brothers who'd helped depose Bligh, William Lawson, the officer who'd valiantly stormed the front door of Government House during the rebellion, and four servants who weren't wealthy enough to be credited as explorers.

The colony was strangely unexcited by the expedition; on the day of their departure, the *Sydney Gazette* ran a lead

---

4   Except for the Aborigines, who crossed the mountains as easily as a settler could cross one of the colony's many Macquarie Streets.

story about a drunk drowning in Sydney Harbour. On their return, the *Gazette*'s account of their successful crossing was overshadowed by an article about a cockfight. Wentworth was philosophical about this muted response, but Blaxland bitched about Macquarie's failure to give him due credit for opening up the continent. Macquarie instead heaped praise on William Cox for building a road over the mountains, naming a river and a pass after him, which was a great honour as geographical features not named Macquarie were in short supply. Blaxland was now incandescent with rage, but Macquarie dismissed his complaints as those of "a lazy, discontented drone". The governor had made himself an enemy.

Macquarie now selected the site for Bathurst, Australia's first inland town, and asked John Oxley to explore the interior. Oxley, who had been appointed surveyor-general because of his "liberal education"[5], had spent his first five years in the job diligently not surveying anything. He spent 1817 and 1818 lost in the Lachlan and Macquarie River marshlands, before emerging to declare that the continent's interior was a vast inland sea. Oxley, who never forgave Macquarie for making him leave the comforts of Sydney, became the pin-up boy for future generations of inept Australian explorers.

AUSSIEMANDIAS

New settlements required new infrastructure, which didn't worry Macquarie because he was an infrastructure kind

---

5   It's amazing how far an Arts degree could get you in 1812.

of guy. It very definitely worried the British Parliament, which couldn't understand why Macquarie was spending its money on new towns for criminals when Britain needed every spare penny to fund its wars against France and America.

Macquarie wasn't only building new towns; he was also renovating the existing ones. When he arrived in Sydney, bark huts leaned higgledy-piggledy against mansions, men and livestock jostled for space on muddy tracks, and the colony's public buildings were in a permanent state of imminent collapse. This was an affront to Macquarie's sense of military order and his wife's sense of aesthetics, so he embarked on an ambitious policy of urban redesign. He tore down houses to straighten streets, insisted that all dwellings be fenced and numbered, decreed that bullocks should not defecate upon his shiny new footpaths, exiled the town's pigs to the newly sprouting suburbs and, to show that the colony had really arrived on the world stage, installed Australia's first flush toilet at his Parramatta weekender. [6]

Despite the repeated urgings of his political masters to curb public spending, Macquarie erected grand edifice after grand edifice, each a monument to his munificence with other people's money. He was pharaoh. He was emperor. He was the grandest of poobahs. He was Aussiemandias

---

6   The French were disgusted by the increasingly popular English custom of installing toilets in residential dwellings, which, flush notwithstanding, they regarded as unhygienic. The French derisively referred to an indoor toilet as "*un lieu à l'anglaise*" or "an English place", which is a possible origin of the term "loo".

and all those who followed him to rule would look on his works and despair.

Macquarie's grand designs were assisted by Francis Greenway, an arrogant, socially maladroit architect who believed that Sir Christopher Wren was a small-town hack (although a couple of his churches were OK). Greenway's genius had not been appreciated in Britain and, in an attempt to escape insolvency, he had forged a document – and so booked himself a one-way ticket to Sydney.

Greenway impressed Macquarie with his certainty about architecture. He told Macquarie that his pride and joy, the Rum Hospital, was crap. The columns were crap, the design was crap and Macquarie was crap for allowing it to be built. So Macquarie set Greenway to work decrapifying Sydney.

The sullen architect did up the hospital at the original builders' expense, earning the eternal enmity of D'Arcy Wentworth. He converted a courthouse into a church and a school into a courthouse. He constructed Gothic forts at Bennelong and Dawes Points, which were useless militarily but looked pretty cool in a detached, brooding kind of way. He erected a miniature Greek obelisk to serve as a reference point for the colony's milestones and a not-so-miniature Greek temple to serve as a water pump for thirsty soldiers. He was thwarted in his desire to include "a giant frieze as a tribute to the winds" in his neoclassical lighthouse at South Head, which included a domed room "for the governor's pleasure" but insufficient space for the troops to be stationed there. The lighthouse he built at Newcastle inexplicably took the form of a Chinese pagoda.

Macquarie's critics labelled his 265 public works "extravagances" and "fugacious toys", but the governor claimed they were necessary to soak up the colony's excess labour. Between 1815, when Napoleon reverted to type,[7] and 1821, the population of New South Wales doubled. All the criminals who had been asked to stand patiently in front of French cannons could now build pretty things for Macquarie.

SHIT APPINS

The progressive settlement of New South Wales was proving unsettling for the First Australians. Some of those who had been moved off their lands hooked up with foreign tribes who dwelled at the fringe of the white man's reach. Others, like Bungaree, moved into the towns.

Bungaree, who had circumnavigated Australia with Flinders and Trim, would paddle out to welcome incoming ships wearing mismatched sailors' clothes and a faux-admiral's hat. The "King of Port Jackson" greeted Macquarie and other new arrivals with a wacky native routine that he had discovered earned him laughs, free food and the occasional coin.

Macquarie regarded Bungaree as a prototype from which he might design a new improved Aborigine. Bungaree was amiable and pleasantly subservient, and his willingness to pander to a stereotype reinforced the colonists' feelings of comfortable superiority. He was a much better role model

---

7   At Waterloo Napoleon did surrender.

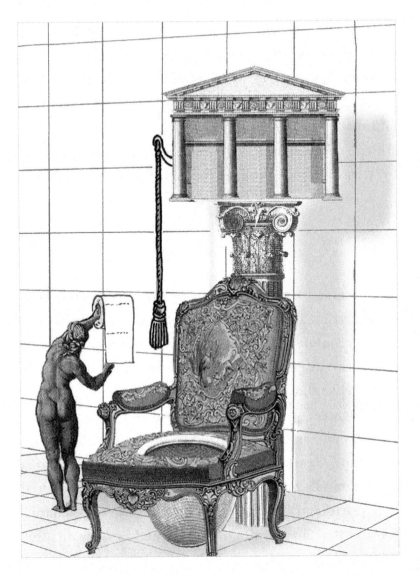

FIG. 10: THE FRANCIS GREENWAY-DESIGNED
MRS MACQUARIE'S CHAIR.

for his people than the brooding Bennelong, who was, quite
frankly, a bit of a downer.

Bennelong had hit the bottle and moved into the garden

of his friend James Squire, Australia's first brewer. [8] He died there in 1813, his affection unconciliated. His obituary in the *Sydney Gazette* illustrated the transformation of the Aborigine, in the colonial mind, from noble to ungrateful savage:

> Of this veteran champion of the native tribe little favourable can be said. His voyage and benevolent treatment in Britain produced no change whatever in his manner and inclinations, which were naturally barbarous and ferocious.

Macquarie, who wanted to be friends with the Aborigines, [9] believed that he could make an "in some Degree useful" people out of Bungaree's stock if he could overcome their "great indolence". He was concerned that Aborigines' lives were "wasted in wandering thro' their native woods" when they might work "as labourers in agricultural employ or among the lower class of mechanics". So he established the Native Institution.

The Institution was devoted to the "Civilization of the Aborigines of both Sexes". It took in children aged four to seven and taught them "Reading, Writing, Arithmetic" and other branches of the learning tree, including "Agriculture"

---

8   Or James Squire and his garden had moved into Bennelong's camp. It's all a matter of perspective.

9   Macquarie even invited Aborigines to his son's birthday parties, although not to the ones that other people were invited to. Lachlan junior loved birthday segregation because he got two sets of presents. He particularly liked the dead birds given to him at his Aboriginal parties, although Government House guests complained about the smell of his collection of badly stuffed parrots.

for boys and "Needle-work" for girls. Macquarie, who promised graduates exciting career opportunities in the dynamic hoeing and sewing industries, ordered:

> That no Child, after having been admitted into the Institution, shall be permitted to leave it, or be taken away by any Person whatever (whether Parents or other Relatives) until such Time as the Boys shall have attained the Age of Sixteen Years, and the Girls Fourteen Years.

The governor hoped that this Borrowed Generation would renounce their tribal ways, marry each other and set up on small acreages, supervised by white managers, in Blacks Town (now the Sydney suburb of Blacktown), a small settlement he had established just for them. His dreams were imperfectly realised, as neither parents nor children had understood the borrowed bit and most students ran away before they could be properly civilised.

Macquarie also experimented on Bungaree, giving him a lovely brass plate to hang around his neck, inscribed with the words "Bungaree: Chief of the Broken Bay Tribe", a tribe and position that Macquarie had entirely made up. The governor then exiled the Bungaree family to a model farm on George's Head. Bungaree didn't see the need to spend all day tilling the earth when he could be bobbing about on the harbour. The farming experiment failed.

Macquarie further attempted to build relationships with his new neighbours by holding an annual state-sponsored corroboree, at which he would distribute trousers, blankets and brass name plates and confer Orders of Merit on well-behaved tribal leaders. He thought everyone was getting on famously until Appin happened.

Three soldiers patrolling the Nepean shot at some Aborigines raiding a cornfield, and killed a boy. The Aborigines speared one of the soldiers and left his mutilated body to be found by his companions. A revenge party marched out and killed an Aboriginal woman and three children. Payback raids killed a number of settlers. The violence escalated.

On 10 April 1816, Macquarie sent out the troops "to inflict terrible and exemplary punishments" on the "hostile Tribes". Any Aborigines found were to be taken prisoner, with those refusing to surrender to be fired upon. The bodies of those killed were to be hanged in trees "in order to strike the greater terror into the Survivors" and the soldiers were to bring in eighteen "good-looking children" for the Native Institution,[10] which was having problems with enrolments.

Captain John Wallis found a recently abandoned campsite in the bush near Appin and, hearing a baby's cry, ordered his men to give chase. They shot at least fourteen Gandangara, mostly old men, women and children. An unknown number of Gandangara threw themselves off a sixty-metre cliff in a frantic effort to escape the soldiers and their dogs. Three dead warriors were beheaded, their bodies left to hang in trees and their heads posted to a venerable Scottish educational institution.

From a governor whose inaugural speech had emphasised that the Aborigines were to be treated with "kindness and

---

10   Macquarie didn't want ugly kids at his show school.

attention", this was hard-core stuff. Macquarie proceeded to kindly and attentively pass laws preventing Aborigines from carrying weapons near settlements or gathering in groups of more than six. Peaceful Aborigines could apply for passports, which they could show to colonists who wanted to shoot them.[11] An amnesty was declared in December 1816, after which Macquarie increased his efforts to Christianise the wayward natives, whom Marsden had refused to minister to on the grounds that "Commerce promotes industry – industry civilisation and civilisation opens up the way for the Gospel."

Marsden's belief that only people interested in buying and selling things could be Christians meant that the Aborigines were spared organised religious instruction until the first missionary arrived in Australia in 1821. The Rev. William Walker, a dour Wesleyan, wasted no time in advising the Aborigines that they were descendants of Ham, the son of Noah whom God had cursed with blackness and condemned to be "a servant of servants to his brothers" (who were a nice pink colour). Judge Barron Field, a founder of the Society for Promoting Christian Knowledge among the Aborigines, mused of his charges, "Perhaps it is better that their name should pass away from this earth". Field's belief in the Aboriginal people's inevitable extinction was embraced by policy-makers for the next century. With friends like Macquarie, Field and Walker, the Aborigines didn't need enemies.

---

11   Unfortunately a passport doesn't have the same range as a musket.

THE PIPE OF MOLLE

There were many bitter opponents to Macquarie's rule but, surprisingly, his problems started with his own regiment, whose officers were outraged that Macquarie expected them to break bread with ex-criminals at Government House dinners. Lieutenant McNaughton was so affronted that he rose from the governor's table in protest.

McNaughton was not, however, opposed to being in the company of convicts in the bedroom. He aggressively pursued one of the colony's many seamstresses and, when a man tried to intervene, beat him to death with a fence paling. McNaughton became one of the convicts he so despised, but to Macquarie's fury received only six months' gaol for manslaughter at court-martial. The governor wrote to the new colonial secretary, Lord Bathurst, seeking an end to officers judging their peers and requesting the recall of the Black Watch. It was Macquarie's willingness to go against his own that, more than anything else, endeared him to the emancipist and convict classes.

The Watch departed in 1814, replaced by the 46th Regiment and its commandant, George Molle, a friend from Macquarie's Indian Army days. However, the governor soon fell out with his old war buddy, who appeared to want to scrape something off the bottom of his shoe every time he saw an emancipist. Matters came to a head when a pipe [12]

---

[12] Pipes were anonymous defamatory writings, commonly written in verse. They were called pipes because the paper on which they were written was rolled into a pipe and inserted into a gap in a wall where it could be found by passers-by. Piping was the trolling of the pre-Facebook era.

was published against Molle. The mocking verse accused him of publicly crawling to Macquarie while backstabbing him, and of being a fat, money-grubbing anti-emancipist bigot and drunken letch who couldn't tell a proper joke. It ended with the words:

> And now, farewell, thou dirty, grov'lling M-ll-
> Go with thy namesake, burrow in thy hole!

The colony's officers offered a £100 reward for the capture of the offending poet, which only served to excite public interest in the pipe and the publication of additional copies. Molle was angered by Macquarie's lack of interest in paying the piper his due, which Molle believed to be a rope and a short, sharp drop. Around this time, William Wentworth suddenly decided he had urgent business in London. During a subsequent inquiry into the pipe, D'Arcy admitted William was its author.

Some officers, with the support of Molle, circulated a pamphlet that wrote of the pipes "issuing from the pens of Men so much our inferiors in rank and situation, that we know them not but among that promiscuous class, which (with pride we speak it) have been ever excluded from intercourse with us". The pamphlet asked Macquarie to "approve and applaud that system of exclusion" and noted that the officers' emancipist-free mess-table was "regarded as the standard of society in this Colony".

Macquarie was angry at this open declaration of class war and apoplectic at the inference that his dining with emancipists was "improper and discreditable". After Molle arrested D'Arcy for the crime of being William's father, Macquarie ordered his erstwhile friend detained until the regiment sailed for home.

THE BROTHERS BENT

Yet Macquarie's problems with the military were nothing compared to those with the judiciary. Ellis Bent, the colony's 26-year-old deputy judge-advocate, was afflicted with constantly weeping eyes and premature baldness, ran to fat and sweated more than an Armenian in a Turkish bathhouse. He suffered from rheumatism and his natural tendency towards stress was exacerbated by a spirited wife who kept falling off horses. Bent loathed the colony with a fervour that bordered on the unholy.

The only thing Bent loathed more than New South Wales was the house Macquarie gave him on his arrival ("a perfect pigstye"). Macquarie dutifully arranged for him to move into one of the grandest residences in the colony. Bent hated it.

Macquarie then gave Bent money to build a combined courthouse and home. Bent built himself a stately manor with a twenty-foot-square ensuite court that he could barely squeeze into. Bent hated it.

Bent then asked for and was granted a large amount of land, which he hated. He sold the property, despite it being illegal to do so, secure in the knowledge that he would let himself off with a stern warning if summonsed to appear before himself.

Bent demanded that Macquarie build him another courthouse, but the obliging governor was stymied by

Bathurst's order to stop wasting Britain's money building things. Bent took this personally. He told Macquarie that he "had shewn a great want of feeling for his attention and personal comfort" and that he "did not consider it necessary to preserve even the external appearance of respect". When people rose in church at the governor's entry, Bent remained obdurately seated. He further insisted that, as a judge, he was not subject to the governor's authority, even though Macquarie's commission made it perfectly clear that he was.

During happier times, Macquarie had recommended Ellis's brother, Jeffery, for appointment as the colony's assistant judge. The cadaverous Jeffery was even more difficult than his brother. Jeffery was insulted that he hadn't been knighted upon his appointment and refused to disembark from his ship until Macquarie arranged a full naval salute to honour his arrival. After landing, he insisted that if the governor didn't have to pay tolls on the Parramatta turnpike, he shouldn't either. "Sir Jeffery", as he was known behind his back, threatened to gaol the tollkeepers who harassed him, and burn down their toll-gate. D'Arcy Wentworth issued a fine for toll evasion, which Jeffery said he didn't have to pay because he was a judge. [13]

The Bents, who had previously employed ex-convicts to do legal work, now decided that emancipist lawyers

---

13   He should have just said someone else was riding his horse. It took two centuries for a brave Australian judge to challenge, on similar grounds, the oppressive road fines imposed on the judiciary by executive government. Unfortunately the Einfeld Defence, as it has come to be known, has been white-anted by non-lawyers who don't properly understand the separation of powers.

could no longer appear in their courts. As there was a critical shortage of non-criminal criminal lawyers, the Bents
closed the courts, throwing the entire justice system into
chaos.

By now Macquarie had had enough and told Bathurst
that if the Bents didn't leave the colony, then he would.
Ellis made things easier by dying, but Jeffery escalated hos-
tilities, claiming that Macquarie had murdered his brother
by providing him with substandard accommodation.

Bathurst finally sacked Jeffery, who had moved in with
Ellis's widow and her horses and had to be formally evicted
from the housing he had long decried. The homeless judge
returned to London to campaign for Macquarie's recall and
his own appointment as governor. He was instead appointed
chief-justice of Granada but was soon suspended from that
position, with Grenada's governor writing, "Peace and
tranquillity can never be restored to this once happy and
united Colony, while Mr Bent is suffered to preside on the
Bench of Justice."

OF UNLIBRARIES AND UNLOBSTERS

Samuel Marsden admired the governor's efforts to curb
immorality. Macquarie had outlawed nude bathing and, as
part of a package of tough Sabbath-breaking laws, prohibited "shooting a neighbour's dog on a Sunday".

Determined to check "the scandalous and perni-
cious custom so generally and shamelessly adopted
throughout the territory of persons of different sexes
cohabiting and living together unsanctioned by the legal

ties of matrimony", Macquarie introduced laws to prevent unmarried women from inheriting their partner's property. Marriage rates skyrocketed. George Johnston, who had quietly slipped back into the colony, finally tied the knot with Esther Abrahams after twenty-seven years of scandalous perniciousness.

But governor and churchman soon fell out over their radically different answers to the emancipist question. Marsden refused to serve as a turnpike commissioner with Thompson and Lord, as associating with ex-convicts would be a "degradation of his sacred office". Macquarie in turn came to regard the preacher as filled with "hypocritical religious cant".

Marsden had raised public funds in England for "a lending library for the general benefit of the inhabitants of New South Wales". The 450 books he purchased included numerous bibles, six sermons on original sin, twelve sermons on the torments of hell, and over a hundred tracts for unhappy women, drunkards, swearers and Sabbath-breakers. There were also lots of books about sheep. The *Sydney Gazette* published an anonymous satirical article pointing out that the books seemed strangely geared towards Marsden's personal interests and querying the library's public character, as it was located on Marsden's country estate, fifteen miles away from any public. Marsden believed the article was written by John Campbell, the editor of the *Gazette* and Macquarie's loyal secretary.

Campbell was later found to be the author of another satirical piece that accused Marsden of stealing from a charity, gun-running, and introducing the Polynesians to "the art of distillation, and that tiny race of animals, which on being boiled, do not prove to be lobsters!"

Marsden, who now made most of his money as a Pacific trader, successfully sued Campbell for the imputation that he got Tahitian girls drunk and gave them crabs. Believing Macquarie had sanctioned the *Gazette*'s attacks, Marsden wrote to his patrons in Britain, accusing Macquarie of providing inadequate facilities at the Female Factory, thereby forcing convict women into prostitution, and condemning the Parramatta Hospital as a place of "drunkenness, whoredom, sickness and death".

Using his position as a magistrate, Marsden launched an investigation into Macquarie's summary flogging of three men who'd trespassed in the Domain after hours. [14] Macquarie shut down Marsden's inquiry and told the turbulent priest he never wished to see him again, unless forced to on public occasions.

Macquarie's enemies were multiplying faster than Rain Man.

THE VIPER NOURISHED

John Macarthur observed Macquarie's emancipist policies from a distance and lamented that they would still

---

14 Macquarie had built a giant wall around the Domain, but "lewd, disorderly men and women" kept on knocking holes in it "for the most indecent improper purposes". The governor, frustrated that his repeated orders to behave properly in Mrs Macquarie's parklands were being ignored, decided to make a public example of the Domain Three. This resulted in a public backlash, as the men were not convicts and should not have been punished without trial.

the birth of the Australian aristocracy that had long been his dream.

Macarthur was not having a good time in Britain. He had become a radical vegetarian, a classic sign of mental instability, and the black dog of depression chewed at his slippers whenever he thought of all he had lost. Yet Macarthur could not return to his wife and sheep, as Castlereagh had ordered Macquarie to try him "as the leading promoter and instigator of the mutinous measures" if he again set foot in the colony.

Bathurst was a more forgiving colonial secretary and allowed Macarthur's return after eight years of exile on condition that he stick to farming, rather than tearing down governors. Macquarie, who got on famously with Mrs Macarthur, took the returning viper into his bosom. He politely received him at Government House, said nice things about his sheep, and was prepared to let bygones be bygones.

Unfortunately Macarthur had other ideas.

THE TIMES THEY ARE A-CHANGIN'

Back in Britain, bleeding-heart liberals were advocating radical social change. There were calls to emancipate Catholics, unchain lunatics, give poor men the vote, abolish capital punishment and, much to the disgust of Sir Joseph Banks, end slavery and animal vivisection. [15] The reformers,

---

15   The wheelchair-bound botanist, still president of the Royal Society and the proud owner of the British Empire's bushiest eyebrows, died of disgust at this new-fangled liberalism in 1820.

many of whom were evangelical Christians, also called for the abolition of transportation and the moral re-education of criminals in purpose-built British gaols.

Henry Grey Bennet MP, one of the leading reformers, regarded Macquarie as a Tory dinosaur. He railed against Macquarie's autocratic powers, his building of "fopperies and follies", his preference for emancipists over free settlers, and his tolerance of moral degeneracy.[16]

Bathurst had already come to the view that Macquarie suffered from "ill considered compassion for convicts" and wanted a scapegoat for his government's transportation policy. Macquarie was his sacrificial ungulate of choice.

Bathurst commissioned John Thomas Bigge, a friend of the Bents, to conduct a wide-ranging inquiry into the affairs of the colony. Bigge was instructed to consider how transportation might once more be made "an object of real terror" and look into the conduct of leading citizens and officials "however exalted in rank or sacred in character", a clear license to gun for Macquarie. Bigge was also given extraordinary powers to make recommendations that Macquarie was compelled to implement, unless he wished to appeal to Mad King George, who was now blind and deaf as well as insane.

Every waking moment of Bigge's two years in the colony was dedicated to tarnishing Macquarie's reputation. He didn't bother to conceal his agenda, starting all interviews

---

16 Bennet's standing as a "moral patriot" took a beating after he propositioned a young male servant at a Belgian health spa. Bennet took less dramatic action than his political enemy, Castlereagh, instead choosing self-exile at Lake Como with the understanding Mrs Bennet.

with "Have you any complaint to make against Governor Macquarie?"

A conga line of suckholes queued at his door to denounce the governor, with Marsden, the Blaxlands and Oxley first in line. Bigge, who expressed "astonishment at the useless magnificence" of Macquarie's building program, even got Francis Greenway to testify against his patron. Greenway, who had previously marketed himself as the colony's architectural visionary, now claimed that he was just the builder. [17]

But it was John Macarthur who played the greatest role in setting the tone of Bigge's three damning reports. Macarthur, while assuring Macquarie of his loyalty, criticised every aspect of his rule, testifying before Bigge that "democratic feeling has already taken deep root in the Colony, in consequence of the absurd and mischievous policy, pursued by Governor Macquarie".

Bigge's reports condemned Macquarie's mollycoddling of convicts and emancipists, accused him of wasting Britain's money, and charged him with neglecting women and the sick. Bigge praised the two-faced Macarthur as an agricultural genius and endorsed his vision for the colony as a feudal aristocracy of "men of real Capital" who would produce wool, wool and wool to keep Britain's feet warm at night.

Macquarie's resignation was finally accepted and he set sail for Britain in 1822 with a shipload of kangaroos for his

---

17   The two-timing architect got his comeuppance, living out his days in a bark hut in a swamp and being buried in an unmarked grave.

friends and patrons.[18] Cheering well-wishers farewelled him from the docks. However unpopular Bennet and Bigge had made him back in Britain, he remained a crowd favourite Down Under.

ABOUT THAT SPARE PENNY ...

Macquarie returned to find himself £500 in debt and under attack from the British Treasury, which couldn't find the receipts for his £10,000 worth of holey dollars and was demanding that he pay for them out of his own pocket. The proud Scot's dreams of living out his days on a comfortable estate were dust. He retired to a tiny leaking house without even a room of his own.

Macquarie didn't much mind his reduced standard of living, as it was traditional for wealthy Scots to live in small windowless hovels, subsisting entirely on porridge and sheep offal. However, he deeply resented not having any money to not spend.

He dedicated the remainder of his life to asking for a pension and rebutting the claims made by Bigge. Although he was politely shunned by MPs in public, his achievements had earned their private respect. Castlereagh, only days before his suicide, took Macquarie to visit the new King.[19]

---

18 Tourists now take toy kangaroos home with them after visiting Australia. Visitors in Macquarie's day, unencumbered by ridiculous quarantine and animal welfare laws, took home the real thing. Macquarie loved kangaroos, probably because they are among the only animals in the world to have inbuilt sporrans.

19 Macquarie paid his respects to the viscount's widow shortly after the letter-opener incident, writing, "She does not appear to suffer from affliction

Bathurst commended him for his "able and successful administration", although he refused to speak these words on the record, and finally gave him a generous pension.

Macquarie did not live to enjoy his golden handshake. He died five weeks later, his passing mourned by a distant people who did not yet know who they were, but whose hearts moved to a beat that was no longer entirely British. In 1824, the year of Macquarie's death, the old men who sat in the shadowed halls of Westminster dusted off the recommendation Macquarie had made seven years earlier and gave a new name to the land he had come to call home.

Australia.

Girt by sea.

---

from the death of her good amiable Lord. She has grown amazingly fat and appears very gay." This was insensitive, as appearing very gay was the cause of Castlereagh's untimely death. Amazingly fat people are also likely to be offended by Macquarie's poor choice of words.

Acknowledgments

I FELL IN LOVE WITH HISTORY AT HIGH SCHOOL, but it was a swords and sandals history populated by scheming Roman senators, Athenian thinkers and hemlock drinkers, and Macedonian warlords who liked it both ways. Australian history, however, bored me to tears. As far as I could make out, it was all about criminals and sheep.

Charles Firth got me interested in Australian history. For fifteen years, I had written nothing but policy documents, ministerial briefings and Parliamentary speeches. It was mid-life-crisis time and I vaguely thought that I might like to do some sketch writing, so I asked Charles to help me package some of my university revue and cabaret material to show to television producers. Charles instead suggested that I work with him and a great young writer, Nich Richardson, on a sketch comedy built around Australian history.

The Complete and Utter History of Australia is the greatest Australian history sketch comedy that has never been made. But in researching and writing for it, I discovered something amazing. Australian history was fascinating. And it was bloody funny.

I began to wonder whether I could write an Australian history that was both accurate and amusing and, in researching whether such a feat had ever been attempted, stumbled across a *Quadrant* article that suggested it may be impossible to write an intentional satire on Australian history. If *Quadrant* suggests something is impossible, then somebody should go out and bloody do it.

I submitted an article on Burke and Wills to the *Monthly* and while its then editor, Ben Naparstek, very politely told me it was not really the *Monthly*'s bag, he passed it on to Black Inc. Black Inc.'s Chris Feik asked if I could write a book in similar style and the rest, as they say, is history. I think it says something wonderful about Australian publishing that an unknown writer can still be afforded this kind of opportunity and I will be forever grateful to Chris and Morry Schwartz for taking a punt.

Chris and Denise O'Dea, my editors, have known when to give me my head and when to rein me in, although I'm sure some readers will think they didn't pull nearly hard enough. They have given me an appreciation of the difference between writing and crafting a book. Their obstinate refusal to publish anything I wrote about Michael Jackson's chimpanzee also does them great credit.

I'd also like to thank a number of historians and social commentators, whom I have found to be delightfully collegiate. Grace Karskens and John Hirst have both answered some of my questions, Stephen Hagan has gracefully allowed me to use a quote on megafaunal extinction that he provided when interviewed for *The Complete and Utter History of Australia*, and Roderick Best of the Fellowship of First Fleeters gave me invaluable advice on primary and secondary source material. John Birmingham and Chris Taylor generously offered their time to read *Girt* before publication. Thanks also to Roger O'Keefe, with whom I co-wrote a revue script in 1993, parts of which can be found in the introduction to Chapter 2 – neither of us can remember who wrote what, but if you find it offensive, I probably wrote it.

Girt is the product of extensive and enjoyable research and I would like to acknowledge some of the authors whose works have significantly informed its development. I love the way Bill Bryson takes history out of the world of dusty academe, and Bryson's *A Short History of Nearly Everything* has informed the style and content of *Girt*. Frank McLynn's *Crime and Punishment in Eighteenth-Century England* is the most entertaining book ever written about whippings, hangings and injecting criminals with the pus of smallpox victims.

Grace Karskens's *The Colony: A History of Early Sydney* is the most beautifully constructed Australian history book I have ever read. Alan Frost's *Botany Bay: The Real Story* and *The First Fleet: The Real Story* provide the most elegant analysis of British settlement. Tim Flannery's *The Future Eaters* and his love affairs with Watkin Tench and Matthew Flinders have helped me to explain who ate all the really big animals and to paint sympathetic portraits (I hope) of two of Australian history's biggest SNAGs.

Henry Reynolds and Bain Attwood have helped me to understand the complex relationships between the first Australians and those that followed: I really hope those two great writers appreciate irony. Kay Daniels, Portia Robinson and Joy Damousi have taught me about the women who became the mothers of a nation, and Patrick O'Farrell's *The Irish in Australia: 1788 to the Present* has enabled me to make more Irish jokes than I would have ever thought possible.

Lovers of biography should read Andrew Tink's *William Charles Wentworth: Australia's Greatest Native Son*; Michael Duffy's *Man of Honour: John Macarthur*; Lyn Fergusson's *Admiral Arthur Phillip: The Man*; Patrick O'Brian's *Joseph Banks: A Life*; Gavin Kennedy's *Captain Bligh: The Man and His Mutinies*; and M.H Ellis' biographies of Macquarie and Macarthur.

Frank Bongiorno's *The Sex Lives of Australians: A History*, John Gascoigne's *Joseph Banks and the English Enlightenment: Useful Knowledge and Polite Culture*, and Miriam Estensen's *Terra Australis Incognita: The Spanish Quest for the Mysterious Great South Land* all deserve honourable mentions. And Keith Windschuttle's *The Fabrication of Aboriginal History* makes an excellent stand for my computer monitor.

A special mention to the Sydney Writers' Room and the writers who inhabit it. It's wonderful that writers have been given a place of quiet collegiality in the heart of Sydney and I would recommend the Room to anyone who is as unproductive writing at home as I am.

Thanks to Kerryn Boland for letting me run away to join the circus; to David Bloustien for coming up with Contiki Too-ral, Li-ooral, Li-addity in developing a television pitch for *Girt*; to David Howarth for inviting me to give a lecture on colonial competition law and for many years of friendship; and to Toni Allan, Sophie Hamley and Michael Fullilove, the Thin White Duke of Australian foreign policy, for giving me tips on the writing and publishing industries. And apologies to Toni, Matthew Mather, James Ward, Mike Jury, Yasmina Searle, Julien "The Baron" Klettenberg, Catriona Carver, Tim Perich, Mary Haines, Rohit Padaonkar and the other Rose Hotel regulars for putting up with all my boring stories about Australian history after the fourth pint of Tiger.

To Ad Long, another Rose Hotel buddy, thank you for being such a wonderful, patient and cheap illustrator. I hope that this is the start of many collaborations to come.

And, most of all, to Alison, Arabella and Dalton, thank you for being you and for helping me to be me.

Index